IMAGES
of America

ITHACA

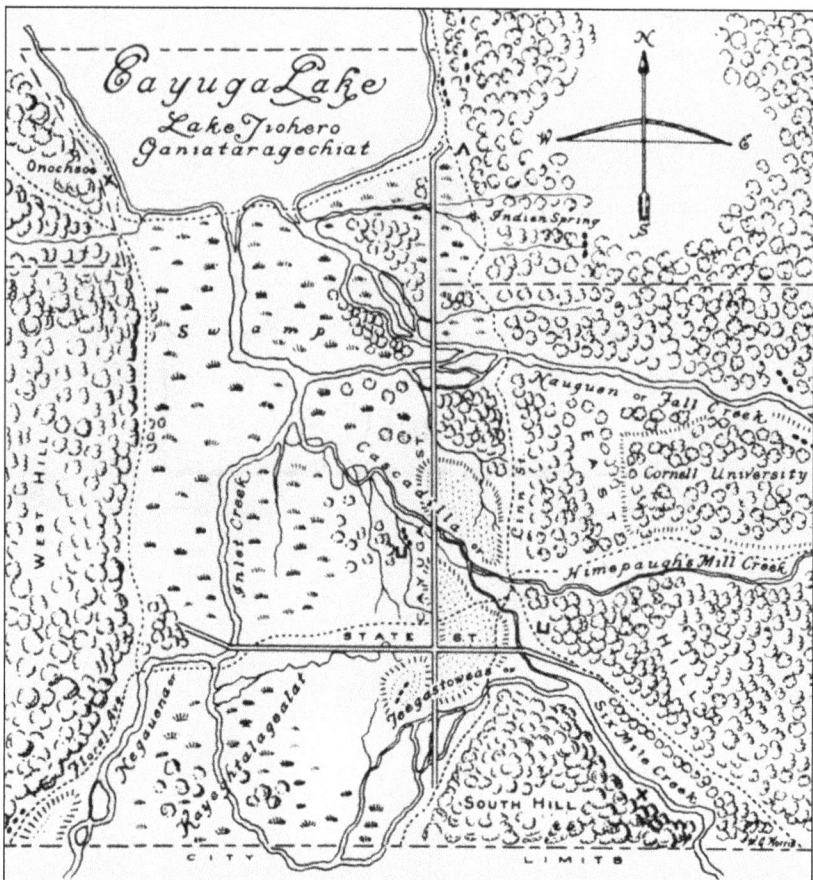

MAP OF ITHACA
showing

ABORIGINAL OCCUPATION, TRAILS, NAMES AND GENERAL APPEARANCE

BEFORE 1790

Laid out within 1944 City Limits - with a few present day land marks indicated.

Legend

▲	VILLAGE SITE	✦ TRACES OF OCCUPATION
✕	CAMP SITE	AREA OF CULTIVATION
Ụ	BURIAL SITE	----- INDIAN TRAILS

This map of pre-1790 Ithaca was drawn by Tompkins County historian and former county clerk W. Glenn Norris. Modern-day streets are included for reference. Native village and camp sites marked include those along the shores of Cayuga Lake and Six Mile Creek; cultivated farmland and footpaths are also noted. (Courtesy of the History Center in Tompkins County.)

ON THE COVER: Ithacans walk in the Six Mile Creek gorge during the first Community Day on May 15, 1917. The event celebrated the opening of Six Mile Glen Park. Thousands of local residents attended, helping to clean up and improve the park, which included school gardens, woods, a baseball field, and other areas. (Photograph by Seth L. Sheldon; courtesy of the History Center in Tompkins County.)

IMAGES
of America

ITHACA

Mary Williams

ARCADIA
PUBLISHING

Published by Arcadia Publishing
Charleston, South Carolina

Library of Congress Control Number: 2011945146

For all general information, please contact Arcadia Publishing:
Telephone 843-853-2070
Fax 843-853-0044
E-mail sales@arcadiapublishing.com
For customer service and orders:
Toll-Free 1-888-313-2665

Visit us on the Internet at www.arcadiapublishing.com

*For my husband, and for the well-being of Ithaca's
ecological and human community.*

CONTENTS

ACKNOWLEDGMENTS

This book was made possible by the History Center in Tompkins County, which preserves and shares the county's history in many ways. Formerly the DeWitt Historical Society, the museum helps visitors learn about local history while making connections with the present. Many thanks to the History Center for support and assistance with this project, including providing access to the museum's extensive photograph collection. All images in this book are courtesy of the History Center in Tompkins County. When known, I have included the names of photographers after image captions.

My appreciation also goes to Arcadia Publishing and my editors for their enthusiasm and helpfulness during the preparation of this book. And thank you to my husband for his unwavering encouragement throughout this project and his editorial skills.

INTRODUCTION

Over the centuries, Ithaca has had many different faces, from lakeside community to college town and from agricultural settlement to industrial center. The area continues to hold different meanings for longtime residents, new arrivals, students, and tourists. This book explores the variety of Ithaca's personas known by locals and visitors over the years and looks back at the earliest—and often forgotten—days of this unique Finger Lakes locale.

Behind the popular "Ithaca is Gorges" slogan, Ithaca's unique landscape sets it apart from other New York communities. Ice Age glaciers contributed to an unusual geology, with creeks flowing through deep gorges to breathtaking waterfalls, which continue to draw tourists from far and wide. Eventually, these creeks and waterfalls powered a variety of mills, and some supplied drinking water to the city.

The first residents of the area are known to have arrived here as long ago as 11,000 B.C. A succession of native peoples lived in the region, hunter-gatherers who favored the shores of creeks and lakes for their camps. By the late 15th century, the Cayuga Nation had built villages and planted crops near Cayuga Lake. Part of today's Ithaca was cultivated for agriculture, and several modern streets were built on or near former Native American footpaths.

The Cayugas are one of the original nations of the Haudenosaunee, sometimes called the Iroquois. As the Revolutionary War developed, the Haudenosaunee and its individual nations remained neutral, although some members were recruited by both sides and fought in the war. In 1779, George Washington ordered the destruction of the Haudenosaunee people, and his forces attacked many villages. Gen. John Sullivan's troops burned Cayuga crops and settlements and killed inhabitants. One of the villages burned was just south of today's city of Ithaca; Coreorgonel was a village of the Tutelo people, adoptees of the Cayuga Nation. In 1789, Governor Clinton made a treaty with the Cayugas, granting them a reservation at the north end of Cayuga Lake. In 1795, the state took this land for use by settlers, and the Cayugas' struggle for a reservation has continued to this day.

Some of the area's first European settlers built rustic homes near Cascadilla Creek about 1789. State surveyor general Simeon DeWitt, nephew of Governor Clinton, planned the early village, which was officially incorporated in 1821. Today, a popular downtown park and historic district are named for DeWitt.

By the early 1820s, the 38-mile-long Cayuga Lake had become a center of both commercial enterprise and tourism. The lake has always been an integral part of Ithaca, known for recreational boating, the steamboat industry, and Renwick (later Stewart) Park along the shore. The Cayuga Inlet was once a highway for boats, and along its banks, until 1925, a community of residents lived in shacks in what was called the Rhine or Silent City.

Early Ithaca was largely a self-sufficient community, and agriculture has always been important, from early Native American crops to present-day family farms. The Ithaca Farmer's Market opened in the early 1970s and often has over 5,000 visitors per day. The earliest business people included merchants, tradesmen, innkeepers, and millers. Daniel Quigg was Ithaca's first merchant. One of the first mills was built at Cascadilla Creek about 1791 by the Yaple family, who were among the earliest European settlers. Elijah Cornell founded one of the village's first factories in 1842, a pottery works on Lake Street. Small, family-owned, and specialized businesses opened on Aurora, State, and other downtown streets, from bakeries to crockery stores.

From agriculture, family mercantiles, and the first mills, local industries expanded and evolved as technology changed. The factories of the Ithaca Gun Company and the Thomas-Morse Aircraft Corporation operated here for decades and became renowned far beyond Ithaca. During World Wars I and II, some companies contributed to the war effort, and in the 1940s, many women went to work in Ithaca's factories at a time when male workers were scarce.

As Ithaca developed and grew, Elijah Cornell's son, Ezra, who had made a fortune in the national telegraph industry, turned his sights to East Hill. There, he and Andrew D. White founded Cornell University in 1865. The university has long been an influential part of the community.

On South Hill, Ithaca College has grown into a well-known liberal arts college, from its modest beginnings downtown in the Rothschild's Department Store building, and later at the Boardman House, when it was known as the Ithaca Conservatory of Music. The conservatory was founded in 1892 by William Grant Egbert.

Ithaca may be well known for its lake, gorges, and educational institutions, but it has other claims to fame. Ithaca's telephone system was one of the first in the country, completed in about 1878. The city installed the first-ever dome dam, completed in 1903, an impressive structure at the municipal water reservoir on Six Mile Creek. The Thomas-Morse Aircraft Corporation produced airplanes for the military during World War I, including the famous S4 (Tommy) Scout. Ithaca was once called the Hollywood of the East, thanks to the area's growing film industry, which began in 1913. The Wharton brothers set up a film studio at Renwick Park the following year, and soon celebrity actors came to town. Ithaca was also home to the first ice cream sundae ever sold.

In 1997, Ithaca was named "the most enlightened town in America" by *Utne Reader* magazine. Enthusiastic patrons of the arts, Ithacans are also known for altruistic and community-minded endeavors. Many of the first residents served as village trustees, mayors, and Common Council members. With a history of social reform and philanthropy, Ithacans were active in the abolitionist movement and later the civil rights movement. St. James African Methodist Episcopal (AME) Zion Church was an important stop on the Underground Railroad, as were local homes. Jane McGraw opened a home for elderly women, and Elizabeth Beebe's mission served the poor of the Inlet area. In 1917, Ithaca came together for the first Community Day in celebration of Robert H. Treman's gift of Six Mile Glen Park. The Southside Community Center opened in its current location in 1938, in collaboration with the national Works Progress Administration. In 1960, students protested segregation when social issues beyond Ithaca became important locally. A look back at Ithaca's earliest days—the landscape, architecture, organizations, and activities—connects today's citizens with those of the past.

One

ITHACA IS GORGES
ITHACA'S UNIQUE AND
DRAMATIC LANDSCAPE

From the earliest human presence in the area, local streams, creeks, and waterfalls sustained life. Early Native American inhabitants along Six Mile Creek were provided with a plentiful source of water and food. Today, the creek continues to supply drinking water to the city. In 1903, a 30-foot dam was completed, and water from the reservoir was routed 4,300 feet through 24-inch iron pipes to the new Purification Works on Water Street. A 60-foot dam was built in 1911, creating the Potters Falls reservoir. Previously, Buttermilk Creek had also provided city water.

Since at least the 19th century, Ithaca's gorges have inspired awe. As proclaimed in the 1866 compilation *The Scenery of Ithaca*, "Rome boasted of her seven hills, from whose throne of beauty she ruled the world. Ithaca makes her boast of seven streams, concerning which she challenges the world. Each of these has a character of beauty peculiar to itself, so that they must all be seen to comprehend the perfect whole." Ithaca's gorges have provided a venue for recreation and rejuvenation for centuries. In the 1860s, one of the village's first photographers, Joseph C. Burritt, captured the beauty of many local glens, often depicting residents relaxing on creek banks or admiring the falls.

These waters have also served essential roles in local industry. One of the earliest mills was the Yaple gristmill on Cascadilla Creek, built about 1791. Among the variety of water-powered mills in Ithaca were also several sawmills along Six Mile Creek. Today, these natural areas are enjoyed by many of the 800,000 visitors to Ithaca and Tompkins County each year, and they continue to be treasured by local residents.

This 1882 bird's-eye-view map of Ithaca portrays the village just six years before the city charter. In the upper left, the Fall Creek gorge cuts through northeast Ithaca along the edge of the Cornell University campus. Cascadilla Creek descends through dense forest at the upper right. Six Mile

A·N·Y·

Creek flows into the village from the map's right border, and in the foreground, the Cayuga Inlet is visible. The steamboat landing is near the end of the Inlet, and the Inclined Plane, part of the railroad line up South Hill heading to Owego, is on the far right.

Captured by Ithaca resident Joseph C. Burritt, Buttermilk Falls is shown here in the 1860s. The wood millwheel indicates a former water-powered mill, one of many along Ithaca's creeks. In the 1866 publication *The Scenery of Ithaca*, the site was described as "the ruins of the quaint old saw-mill at their base." Burritt was one of the area's first major photographers and one of the most prolific.

A path and railing lead the way up the trail from the base of Buttermilk Falls. Nearby was once the Tutelo village called Coreorgonel, meaning "Where we keep the pipe of peace." This settlement of Cayuga Nation adoptees was destroyed by soldiers in the Sullivan Campaign of 1779.

Two men rest on opposite sides of Buttermilk Creek gorge in this c. 1860s photograph. Behind them is the Fourth Falls. The late Devonian Age geologic structure of the gorge's shale walls can be seen in detail. The creek descends 600 feet along the east side of the Cayuga Lake valley. (Photograph by Joseph C. Burritt.)

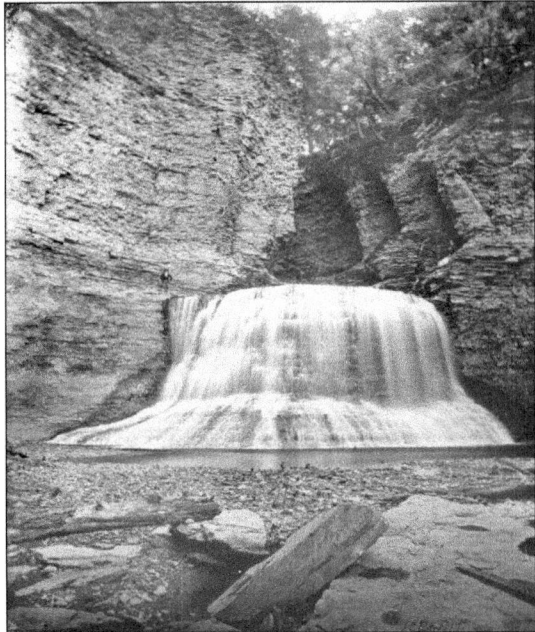

A man stands above and to the left of Pulpit Falls at Buttermilk Creek in this 1860s image. Buttermilk Creek supplied drinking water to the city of Ithaca until the early 1900s. In later years, the magnificent Buttermilk Glen was used as a backdrop for the silent film *The Perils of Pauline*, a Wharton Studios production. (Photograph by Joseph C. Burritt.)

Four women grace a waterfall along Buttermilk Creek in this portrait from the 1860s. This glen has long been a destination for Ithacans seeking recreation. It was not until 1924 that Buttermilk Falls State Park officially opened, comprising 154 acres of forest, gorges, and waterfalls. A manmade lake is also located within the park. (Photograph by Joseph C. Burritt.)

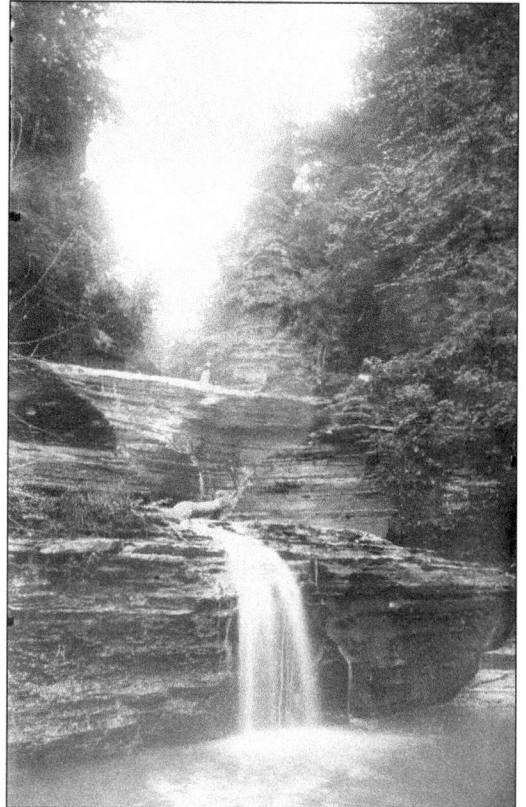

A woman standing above the falls gives scale to this photograph of Buttermilk Creek gorge from the late 1800s. The towering shale rock formation is known as Pinnacle Rock, one of many spectacular natural features in the gorge. The 40-foot-high formation was created by erosion from the creek flowing around the shale.

This image of Ithaca Falls shows Fall Creek at flood stage. After heavy rains, particularly in spring, the falls have long been an impressive sight. Above the falls, the Stewart Avenue bridge spans the creek. Factory Street was renamed Stewart Avenue in about 1888, in honor of Mayor David Barnes Stewart.

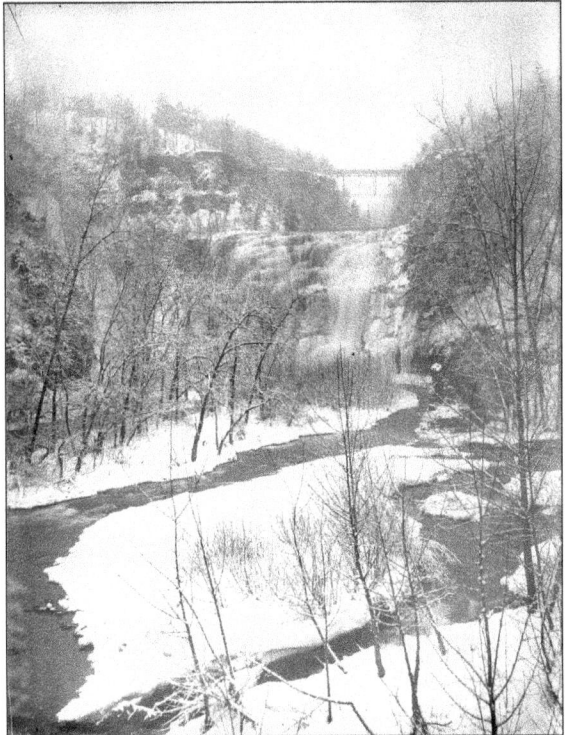

Ithaca Falls is partially frozen in this winter scene. The falls flow over part of the Ithaca Formation of ancient rock. Fall Creek has historically been used for both recreation and industry. By 1813, the falls were already being used for waterpower at the plaster and carding mill owned by Phineas Bennett.

Ithaca Falls appears nearly dry in this summer scene. In times of drought over the years, water has stopped flowing altogether. In 1840, Jeremiah S. Beebe sold the site's gristmill to the Ithaca Falls Woolen Manufacturing Company, which converted it to a woolen cloth mill. Here, water descends about 150 feet. In the mid-1800s, Ithaca Falls was considered the largest waterfall in New York state, after Niagara Falls.

This striking photograph of Ithaca Falls was taken in the 1860s. The forested and secluded scene evoked the following sentiment from author F.W. Clarke in 1869: "Had Ithaca but one ravine, thousands of tourists would visit it, but, having many, they remain almost unknown." (Photograph by Joseph C. Burritt.)

By 1817, when the first gristmill was built on Fall Creek, water was routed through a wood flume, held in place by beams attached to the gorge walls. The flume pictured here was part of Ezra Cornell's system, completed in 1832, which provided waterpower for mills near Ithaca Falls. (Photograph by Joseph C. Burritt.)

A streetcar and a horse-drawn buggy can be seen on the Stewart Avenue bridge, high above the Fall Creek gorge. The Ithaca Street Railway Company began to operate the trolley system about 1887, although this line was not complete until the bridge was built about 1900. The first trolley line was on State Street; additional routes went to Cornell University and East Hill in the 1890s.

Skaters can be seen on Beebe Lake on the Cornell University campus. Below the lake, Triphammer Falls and the Hydraulic Laboratory are visible. In the 1830s, long before founding the university, Ezra Cornell built a dam across Fall Creek, forming the lake as a reservoir for use in dry seasons. Cornell was a mechanic and manager of Jeremiah S. Beebe's plaster and flour mills down the hill at Ithaca Falls.

A new dam was built on Fall Creek above Triphammer Falls in 1898. Cornell University also built the Hydraulic Laboratory there the same year, as a project of the College of Civil Engineering. The college's director, Estevan Antonio Fuertes, originally from Puerto Rico, had advocated for the laboratory, which furthered research in water flow. The reservoir supplied water to campus and powered the electric plant in the gorge.

People along the suspension bridge over Fall Creek gorge pause to observe swimmers below enjoying the shallow creek on a summer day in the early 1900s. The gorge was popular among townspeople and students from the nearby Cornell campus.

The Sixth Fall on Cascadilla Creek flows toward the village below as a man looks on from above, on the right. The site was near Willow Pond. The Cascadilla gorge passed William's Mill at the center of Ithaca and later became part of the Cornell University campus. (Photograph by Joseph C. Burritt.)

Two men sit on the rocky bank of Green Tree Falls on Six Mile Creek in this image from the 1860s. Also called Mineral Spring Falls, the site provided visitors a firsthand view of the creek's distinctive geological features along the gorge. The Six Mile Creek gorge, like others in Ithaca, was formed when Ice Age glaciers retreated 10,000 years ago, and streams slowly began to erode the surrounding rock. (Photograph by Joseph C. Burritt.)

Men work in the Six Mile Creek bed during construction of the 60-foot Potters Falls Dam, completed in 1911. As shown here, water was diverted by a flume to allow for the construction. It was the second major dam on the creek, and provided a second reservoir for the city's drinking water.

Two

EARLY ITHACANS
EARLIEST IMAGES OF ITHACANS
AND THEIR HOMES

Before Ithaca was officially named, the area was known by other designations. After the first Europeans arrived, they called the valley The Flats, or Markle's Flats, after influential settlers Abraham and Henry Markle. It was even known as Sodom in certain circles, based on its reputation as an unruly, amoral frontier town. By 1790, the state's surveyor general, Simeon DeWitt, had surveyed the 1.5-million-acre swath of Haudenosaunee land to the east of Seneca Lake called the Military Tract. Many Revolutionary War veterans received 600-acre allotments. Township number 22, which included the area that would become Ithaca, was called Ulysses. As early as 1802, DeWitt had placed the name Ithaca on his official New York state map. Ithaca's final name has most often been attributed to DeWitt, who, at one time, owned a substantial part of the settlement and adjacent areas. On March 16, 1821, the town of Ithaca was officially organized, separating from the town of Ulysses. Within its boundaries was the village of Ithaca, incorporated on April 2 of that year.

Among Ithaca's first European settlers, the Dumond, Hinepaw, and Yaple families travelled from Kingston, on the Hudson River, to Ithaca in 1789. Peter Hinepaw built his family's cabin near the site of today's Christian Science Church at Cascadilla Creek. The Dumonds and Yaples settled near the base of today's East State Street, close to the future site of the Cowdry house. In 1795, the Dumond and Yaple families moved near Buttermilk Creek, after discovering that they did not hold legal title to their land. Other early settlers, arriving between about 1788 and 1791, were the McDowells and Woodworths, who built cabins near today's Cayuga Street at its junctions with Seneca and Buffalo Streets.

As Ithaca grew over the years, some residents, such as John Barden, had come to work for the railroads or other industries. Others, descendants of early settlers, including Emeline Quigg, simply remained.

This 1840 map of Ithaca was the first to include the location of buildings in the village. In the 1840s, Ithaca's population grew only little. But, during this time, commerce began to increase and public works projects improved the young village. The map shows a cotton factory on East Hill, near Cascadilla Creek just above Eddy Street. Factory Street has not yet been renamed Stewart Avenue, and today's State Street was called Owego Street. The steamboat landing is shown on the Cayuga Inlet, and the State Pier juts out onto Cayuga Lake from the end of Lake Avenue. The Ithaca and Owego Railroad is also visible on the map, beginning at the Inclined Plane on South Hill. Just two years after the map was published, the railroad failed and was sold.

When Ira Tillotson moved to Ithaca in 1809, he soon became an active member of the Ithaca community. Born in Connecticut in 1783, he held several important positions in Ithaca, including serving as the village's ninth president. Tillotson was also an architect, builder, and surveyor who designed the Dutch Reformed, First Methodist, and Presbyterian churches. He died in 1858 in Michigan, where he resided in his later years.

Emeline Quigg lived from 1815 until 1908 and resided at 115 East Seneca Street. When she died, she was the oldest native of Ithaca. Her father, David Quigg, from New Hampshire, was Ithaca's first merchant. Miss Quigg, as she was known, was a member first of the Dutch Reformed Church and then its successor, the Congregational Church. She was known as a dignified, graceful woman with many friends.

Family members pose with their horse and buggy at the old Ackley residence. Henry Ackley built the Federal-style home just after 1812 at the northwest corner of Cayuga and Seneca Streets, the future site of the Women's Community Building. The house was moved in the 1870s to 615 West Seneca Street. Ackley was involved in building the Clinton Block and Clinton House in 1830. (Photograph by Joseph C. Burritt.)

Born in Sharon, Schoharie County, New York, in 1810, Adam S. Cowdry moved with his family to Ithaca in 1822. Ten years later, he married Mary Frances Riley, who was from England. In addition to running his father's carriage and blacksmith shop, Cowdry became a wealthy businessman and later served as a member of Eureka Fire Company Number Four. (Photograph by Charles H. Howes.)

Family members pose at the home of coachmaker Adam S. and Mary Cowdry. Adam served as a village trustee for 14 years and was elected 33rd president of Ithaca for two one-year terms, 1873 and 1874. Later known by the name of his daughter, Belle, the house was built in 1831 by Jacob McCormick at the foot of East Hill. Located at 408 East State Street, the house is now a bed-and-breakfast inn. Cowdry's carriage shop was located just down the hill at 105–107 North Aurora Street in the 1850s. Born in 1838, Belle Cowdry went on to study Latin and mathematics at the Ithaca Academy. She had many suitors but resisted the pressures of her time and never married. She lived in the Cowdry mansion until her death at age 84.

In 1818, Horace Mack (1799–1855) moved from Cooperstown, New York, to Ithaca. He later co-owned Fall Creek Flouring Mills with John James Speed. Mack owned the Irish Settlement on the road to Newfield, but he lived at 115 West Green Street. Later, he built a house at 105 West Green Street and lived there with his wife, Ann Eliza (Ferris) Mack, and their children. He served as 20th president of Ithaca. (Photograph by Charles H. Howes.)

Edgemont, the home of William Hance, is depicted in this illustration from the border of an 1853 map of Tompkins County. Prominent citizens such as Hance paid to have their homes and businesses included on the map. He was elected as a trustee of the village of Ithaca in 1828, under Pres. Charles Humphrey, serving until 1831, and again in 1834 with Pres. Wait T. Huntington.

Elsie Brooks was born into slavery near Harper's Ferry, West Virginia. In 1811, she was brought to Danby by her mistress, Amy Furness. After slavery was abolished in New York in 1827, Elsie moved to Ithaca. She married Jacob Brooks, who died about 1835. She lived next to and attended St. James AME Zion Church. Remembered by friends as an influential woman with a powerful voice, she died in 1875. (Photograph by Jefferson Beardsley.)

Alson Dean was an artist and woodcarver who lived at 88 Linn Street. Born in 1822 in Manlius, Onondaga County, New York, Alson arrived in Ithaca in 1842 and focused on his art despite ill health. Ezra Cornell was one of his patrons and encouraged his work. Dean created intricate mechanical models, from ships and sawmills to mythical creatures, which he exhibited and sold in his own museum.

Lafayette Treman was known as a gentle and engaging churchgoer with an interest in the arts and industry. He was a supporter and director of the Lyceum Theater, built in 1893 on South Cayuga Street. Treman married Eliza Mack, daughter of Horace Mack, the 20th president of the village of Ithaca. (Photograph by C.H. Howes.)

This home on Geneva Street was built about 1840. In 1857, Eleanor Mack signed over the deed to her son-in-law Lafayette Treman, husband of Eliza (Mack) Treman. Lafayette served as assessor during his father-in-law's term as village president and became a director of the Tompkins County Bank. He later became president of the bank, serving until his death in 1900. (Photograph by Joseph C. Burritt.)

In 1868, John Gauntlett was the first naturalized citizen elected village president. He was born in England in 1813. A young apprentice at the Mack and Andrus book bindery, he became foreman, then partner. In 1839, he married Susan Burritt, sister of Joseph C. Burritt. After her death, he married Mary Jane Burritt of Connecticut. Later Gauntlett owned a drugstore with his son and Arthur B. Brooks. (Photograph by C.H. Howes.)

This Federal-style residence, built in 1848 on East State Street, was home to the Gauntlett family and later belonged to Elmer Wanzer. By the 1940s, the Eagles building, built by the Fraternal Order of Eagles, stood on the site. John E. Gauntlett stands in the foreground, while his father, John, is seen behind the fence. The elder Mrs. Gauntlett and her daughter are believed to be among the women.

John Barden, born in New Hampshire in 1825, came to Ithaca in 1849 and helped build the railroad to Owego. He worked for the Delaware, Lackawanna and Western Railroad, was a shipping agent near the steamboat landing, and then a passenger train conductor. He married Abbie Shaw of Owego and built a house at 423 East Seneca Street. Barden was elected second mayor in 1889. (Photograph by C. H. Howes.)

Cliff Park, the home of the Hon. Josiah Butler Williams and his wife, Mary (Hardy) Williams, was featured in this engraving on the border of an 1853 map of Tompkins County. A banker and state senator, Williams had this stone house built in the 1840s on West Hill between Hector and Elm Streets, above the Cayuga Inlet.

Joseph C. Burritt was born in 1817, after his parents arrived from Connecticut. He joined his father's jewelry business (Burritt, Clark, and Company) opposite State Street's Ithaca Hotel, and later became one of Ithaca's first photographers in the early 1860s. He and his wife, Hetty Marie Lord, lived on North Albany Street between Seneca and Buffalo Streets, and they had four children. After Hetty's death, Joseph married Julia Atwater.

Family members pose for a portrait outside the Frederick Brooks homestead in this collodion photograph, taken about 1863. The house stood at 32 North Albany Street on the corner of Buffalo Street. Brooks, a cousin of Joseph C. Burritt, owned a hat shop at 40 East State Street. (Photograph by Joseph C. Burritt.)

Capt. Doctor Tarbell is pictured at the headquarters of the Third Corps, Army of the Potomac, during the Civil War. Tarbell's first name really was Doctor. Originally from Groton, he settled in Ithaca with his wife, Mary Lucy (Conant) Tarbell, after the war. He was elected Tompkins County clerk and worked in the insurance business.

Thomas G. Miller owned a business selling stationery, paper, and school supplies in the Blood Building on North Tioga Street. First called Enz and Miller, the business was founded in 1878 on East State Street by Miller and Frank J. Enz, former employees of the Andrus and Church book bindery. Miller was also a manufacturer and owned a paper mill. He lived at 219 South Albany Street.

Adelbert H. (Del) Mackey's wife and his mother pose behind a fence with Mrs. Edward J. (Ann) Curtis in this c. 1880 photograph. The Curtises and the Mackeys lived here at 27 (later 127) Linn Street. The front part of the house was moved from the northeast corner of Seneca and Aurora Streets. Edward and Del were employed as painters.

The Hon. Edward S. Esty was the president of the board of education from 1874 to 1890. A manufacturer, Esty lived at 36 North Geneva Street. In 1885, he gave a parcel of land to the Ladies' Union Benevolent Society. The Children's Home for orphans was built on that West Seneca Street property.

Martin and Helen Freer flank their son William in the late 1800s in this photograph taken outside their home on North Meadow Street in Ithaca's West End. Martin had worked as a laborer, liveryman, butcher, and hostler. From about 1884 to 1889, William was employed as a bellboy at the Clinton House.

Members of the Green family pose in front of a South Hill duplex at 226–228 (formerly 58, 1, and 2) Columbia Street. Emeline Green lived at 228 from about 1892 to 1906, while a number of tenants lived at 226, including Henry Sutton and John J. Seager. The younger woman pictured here is Dorothy Green. The woman seated is believed to be Emeline.

A tree lies on its side after being uprooted during a storm in about 1895. Elosia Fish Haseman is in the center of the group, viewed from South Geneva Street. Shown are the grounds of the Jane L. Hardy house at 27 West Clinton Street, which later became the Red Cross headquarters. Behind is the Frank H. Romer home, and to the left rear is the Roger B. Williams house.

William and Emma Horton Krum stand before the porch at their home, Locust Villa, in about 1900. The residence was the last house on the right side of Coddington Road, named after the Coddington family. The home stayed in the Krum family for many years. In the 1930s, Clarence Krum was still living in the house.

The Cayuga Inlet neighborhood was known as the Rhine when this photograph was taken in 1895. Pictured here are the homes of Dido Stephens, Sandy Gardner, and John Oatman. The residents built their homes along the Inlet, but they did not own the land. Houses on West Hill are visible in the distance.

Inlet resident Mrs. Sate Letts stands in the foreground at the home of Sandy Gardner on October 19, 1905. The Rhine was also called Silent City. Like the Gardner house, other Inlet abodes were made of scrap lumber. Many locals looked down on the Inlet residents, but others reached out to this community.

Governor Right, a resident of the Rhine community along the polluted Cayuga Inlet, is pictured here about 1900. The residents were poor, often only seasonally employed due to their dependence on factory work. In 1925, the last eight Rhine residents were forced to move to houses on Floral Avenue when the city began the Inlet beautification campaign.

The Edward G. Wyckoff family home is photographed in 1901 during a business gathering of Wyckoff's typewriter industry associates and other guests. Architect William H. Miller designed the Colonial Revival house, which was built at the corner of Highland and Thurston Avenues on the highest lot in Wyckoff's new development, Cornell Heights.

At left, Elfrieda (Hochbaum) Pope stands between her husband, Paul, on the right, and an unidentified man on their new lot at 110 Overlook Road in Cayuga Heights. Taken about 1906, the photograph also shows the van Pelt home in the distance. Ground breaking for the Pope's home is captured below in 1907. The Popes watch from the sidewalk as a team of horses pulls a plow and a man digs into the snow-covered soil. The O'Connell house is on the left. During construction, the Popes lived in a small, temporary house next door, borrowed from Cornell University.

Family members stand in the snow outside the completed Pope home at 110 Overlook Road in 1912 or 1913. The Popes lived in the same house for several decades. By 1954, Elfrieda (Hochbaum) Pope published a novel called *The Stain*, set on the Cornell University campus. Pope's husband, Paul, was a professor.

This multigenerational portrait of the Roscoe D. Brown family was captured in 1909 on the steps of their home at 305 East Marshall Street. Roscoe was a photographer and worked at Seth L. Sheldon's studio on East Avenue. At that time, East Avenue was also the site of several Cornell University faculty residences.

Solomon Chapman and his wife, Elizabeth (Lizzie), stand before their home at 520 West Clinton Street about 1910. Solomon was a cooper in Fred Middaugh's barrel factory at 115–117 East Clinton Street. He married Lizzie after the death of his first wife. In the background at left is the steeple of St. James AME Zion Church.

Ellen D. Belcher, widow of Isaac Belcher, stands among the flowers in her garden. To the right is her home at 216 Cleveland Avenue, where she lived during the 1920s. Formerly called Wheat Street, the name changed in 1908 at the request of the residents, who wished to honor the memory of former United States president and New York state governor Grover Cleveland.

Three

MADE IN ITHACA
AGRICULTURE, BUSINESS, AND INDUSTRY

During the 19th century, Ithacans found livelihoods, sustained their families, and built wealth in a variety of ways. Many established farms, producing food to consume and sell at market. Early on, farms could be found in the village, then in the city, as well as within the larger town boundaries. Today's Ithaca Farmer's Market, which opened in 1973, is the most recent of many farm markets over the decades.

The railroad industry also became an important part of commerce in Ithaca. The Ithaca and Owego line opened in 1834, originally drawn by horses. Railroads were used to carry passengers and freight, including salt, plaster, and coal. East Hill had its own passenger depot, built for the Elmira, Cortland and Northern Railroad in 1876, five years after the lines were in place. The first West End train station was replaced about 1919 by a more permanent structure, which is now used as the bus depot.

Early Ithaca industries included mills and factories, such as the Fall Creek Milling Company, which opened in 1830. The mill produced flour and paper. Plaster mills and sawmills were in place by 1817. Otis Eddy's cotton mill, which appeared on the 1840 village map, was built near Cascadilla Creek in 1827. In 1846, Cascadilla Mills was built as a gristmill. A cider mill was constructed in Free Hollow, today's Forest Home neighborhood. Other early products manufactured in Ithaca included woolen fabric, stoneware pottery, and farm implements.

Merchants, tradesmen, and small businesses operated throughout downtown. The earliest were carpenters, coopers, and hatters. Later there were grocery stores, including McWhorter's and Atwater's, and family-owned bakeries on Aurora and Corn Streets. By the early 1900s, businesses tied to national markets were established. Companies included Thomas-Morse Aircraft, Morse Chain, Ithaca Gun, and National Cash Register.

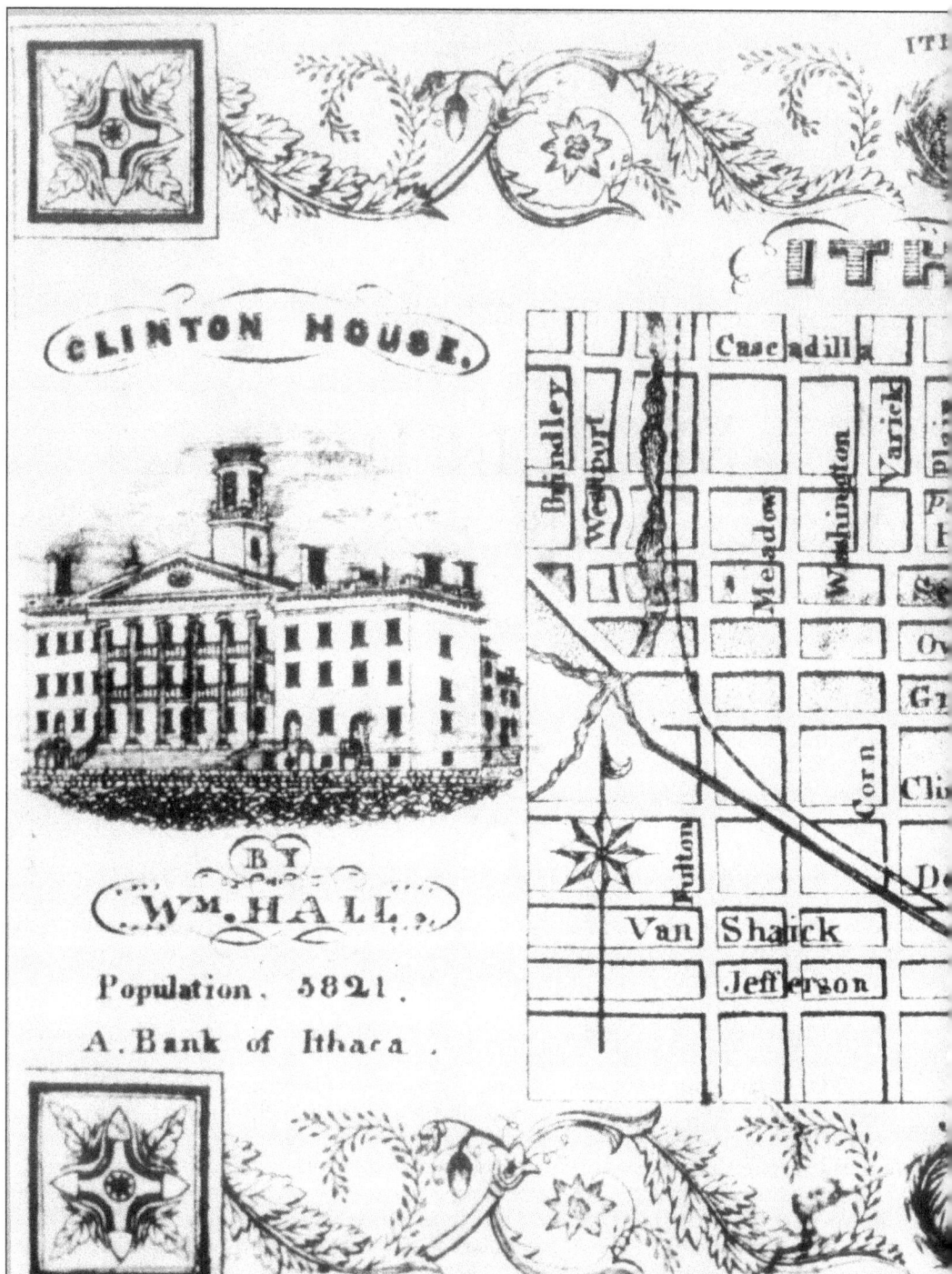

The Clinton House and the Ithaca Hotel are featured on this early village map. Built in 1809 by Luther Gere, the original Ithaca Hotel was a three-story wood building. When it burned in 1871, a four-story brick structure replaced it the following year. Located on East State Street, it was a popular hotel and restaurant for many years. The building was demolished in 1967 as part

(ITHACA HOTEL.)

BY
S. D. THOMPSON.

B. Tompkins Co. Bank

C. Merchants and Farmers

of Ithaca's urban renewal projects. The Clinton House, a Greek Revival–style hotel on North Cayuga Street, was completed in 1830 in a partnership between Henry Ackley and his associates Jeremiah S. Beebe and Henry Hibbard. Today it is occupied by a charter high school.

The Clinton House was brimming with activity on this day in the late 1800s. The hotel became known as the finest west of the Hudson River. The grand building, which may have been designed by Ira Tillotson, had 151 rooms. The enormous columns were made from ancient oak trees disguised by layers of brick and stucco.

Tompkins County Bank on East State Street is captured in this 1853 engraving. Founded in 1836, the institution became a national bank 30 years later. During the Panic of 1857, businessman Josiah Butler Williams pushed a wheelbarrow full of silver and gold into the bank to ease the worries of customers. The bank merged with the Ithaca Trust Company to become Tompkins County Trust Company in 1935.

The pottery works at Fall Creek was located at the corner of Lake Street and Railroad Avenue (now East Lincoln Street). The stoneware manufacturer was run by James Macumber and others over the years. The business was founded in 1842 by Elijah Cornell, a potter from DeRuyter and father of Ezra, founder of Cornell University. (Photograph by Joseph C. Burritt.)

In this early view of Ithaca, Cayuga Lake can be seen in the background. The pottery works is at left. A weaver named A. Davison worked in a small brick house nearby on the corner of Falls Street. The mounds in the foreground are likely straw, possibly used by the pottery works in the manufacturing process. (Photograph by Joseph D. Eagles.)

Timothy Shaler Williams built the Cascadilla Mills in 1846. An earlier gristmill had been built near the site about 1791 by Jacob Yaple, one of Ithaca's first European settlers. Williams's son Howard took ownership of Cascadilla Mills in 1858, and managed the mill for about 30 years. The Williams family owned land on both sides of Cascadilla Creek.

L.S. McWhorter's grocery store on East State Street was in the McWhorter block, built in the 1860s and later known as the Baldini Building. The two families owned the building, which was located on the northeast corner of Cayuga and State Streets, for over 100 years. The store was later succeeded by another grocer, then shoe stores, including Williams Shoes, opened by William Baldini in 1949.

Andrus and Church, a book bindery and bookstore, was located at 143 East State Street. William Andrus had been a traveling bookseller in Connecticut until 1824, when he joined Ebenezer Mack's print shop and bindery, which had many names and owners over the years. Mack was also a publisher of the *Seneca Republican*, which became the *Ithaca Journal* in 1823. The two men bought the East State Street property in 1831. Mack died in 1849. After Andrus's death 20 years later, his son partnered with William A. Church. Following an 1871 fire, the pair constructed a new building on the site and conducted business until 1929, when Church moved his printing business next door. In this c. 1910 photograph, employees pose before the entrance. Some of those identified include Theodore F. and Fred W. Hasenjager (both printers), Georgia W. Cole, Nellie Miller, and Katherine Seamon. Later, the Home Dairy operated from this site; it is now a cafe and coffee shop.

Two employees are shown among dishes, oil lamps, and children's wagons for sale at George Rankin and Son's Crockery Store in about 1875. The shop at 42 East State Street was known for its china, crockery, and glassware and was one of many small businesses in the village.

City officials stand outside the Ithaca Savings Bank, built on Tioga Street in 1887. After this building was damaged by fire, a new structure was built in 1924. The bank formed in 1868 on East State Street and Ezra Cornell was the first president. In 1878, it moved to a house at the site pictured here, once the home of Ezra's son Alonzo, and where Ezra died in 1874. The house was demolished for the building shown here.

The Van Natta's gristmill was built above Six Mile Creek on Giles Street in the 1880s. Using waterpower at the site of their dam, brothers James and John E. Van Natta ground grain and sold it at their feed business just up the creek. By 1903, the mill was converted to a water-pumping station for the city's new water supply, piped from the creek's reservoir farther upstream.

Lehigh Valley No. 67 travels along the tracks on Ithaca's West End. East Hill is visible in the distance. The Lehigh Valley Railroad took over many small lines in 1890, including the Geneva, Ithaca and Sayre, and assumed control of the Elmira, Cortland and Northern Railroad in 1896.

McClune Cycle Company, on the corner of South Cayuga and Green Streets, sold and repaired bicycles, sewing machines, and typewriters. The sign shown here about 1903 advertised lock and safe work. Fred A. McClune became Ithaca's first automobile dealer, and by 1907, he ran the Ithaca Automobile Company and McClune's Bicycle Exchange from a building near today's Holiday Inn on South Cayuga Street. (Photograph by Bill Pyle.)

The Modern Method Laundry was owned by John Reamer at 210 East Seneca Street. The business's slogan was "We make your linen live." Designed by Gibb and Waltz and built in 1907, the structure was also occupied by Clarence Head's shirt factory. Before 1907, the livery of the Tompkins House Hotel had been located on the site.

This cartoon was published as part of a series in the *Ithaca Daily Journal* on May 11, 1908. A caricature of Ebenezer Mack Treman is shown, while a band plays behind him, representing his patronage of Patrick Conway's Ithaca Band. Ebenezer was born in 1850 and attended Cornell University in its inaugural class. Like his father, Lafayette, Treman became president of Ithaca Gas Light Company.

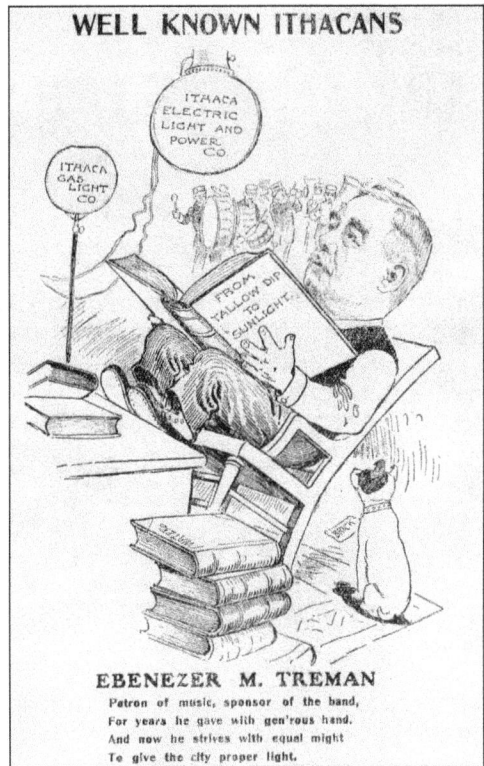

WELL KNOWN ITHACANS

ITHACA ELECTRIC LIGHT AND POWER CO.

ITHACA GAS LIGHT CO

FROM TALLOW DIP TO SUNLIGHT

EBENEZER M. TREMAN

Patron of music, sponsor of the band,
For years he gave with gen'rous hand,
And now he strives with equal might
To give the city proper light.

The Scott Brothers wholesale bakery was located at 838 North Aurora Street in the Fall Creek neighborhood during the early 1900s. Albert F. Scott and Lewis J. Scott owned the business and Leslie N. Scott worked as a driver. Albert lived at 302 Falls Street, while Leslie and Lewis lived at 912 North Tioga Street. Lewis was also affiliated with the Ithaca Cement Block Company.

Warner's Store, selling wallpaper at 322 West State Street, is pictured here about 1910. The owner was Harry Warner, who lived at 810 North Tioga Street. Fred H. Atwater's grocery store was next door at 320 West State for several years. At that time, downtown Ithaca was bustling with small, family-owned businesses such as Warner's.

The Greek-American Fruit Company store is pictured next door to the Salvation Army. Shop owners pose at the front entrance. By 1898, the first Greek immigrants moved to the Ithaca area, including John Chacona, who owned a candy shop. Others opened grocery and fruit stores and restaurants.

Men load hay on a horse-drawn wagon in Bryant Park in 1910. The house, 201 Fairmount Avenue, belonged to Cornell University professor Walter B. Carver. At the time, agriculture was still part of life in Ithaca. In the background, the English Lumberyard and houses on Cornell Street are visible. Bryant Park was a subdivision built on the former Bryant farm beginning about 1908.

Workers at Burns' Bakery pause for a photograph while dough rises in a wood trough. William L. Burns owned the bakery at 110 North Corn Street in the early 1900s and lived nearby at 510 West Seneca Street. Paul J. Burns also joined the business and boarded at 501 West State Street. (Photograph by Seth L. Sheldon.)

A billboard for Barney Seamon's store at 146–148 East State Street depicts a trolley with passengers, advertising a convenient way to travel to the downtown shop. The business sold clothing, shoes, and furnishings in the early 1900s. Seamon lived in a boardinghouse at 120 East Seneca Street.

Ithaca tinsmiths pose for a portrait during a parade in the 1910s. James Henry "Red" Moore stands among the group, third from the left. Behind them is the old Ithaca Savings Bank, designed by William H. Miller, and built on the corner of Seneca and Tioga Streets.

Employees of the Thomas-Morse Aircraft Corporation are pictured at the factory during World War I. The airplanes being constructed in this photograph were likely for the military, as the company was contracted to build planes for the US Army during the war. Thomas-Morse aircraft became well known beyond Ithaca.

DH4 planes are shown with Thomas-Morse Aircraft Corporation employees at the factory. The airplanes were being converted to DH4B models after World War I. The fuel tanks and cockpits were moved to modify the planes for postwar use. Ernest Crance is the only identified employee, fifth from right, behind the second plane.

A train with a Pullman car sits at the Ithaca station on the West End. This view shows the depot on the left. The Delaware, Lackawanna and Western Railroad Company built the brick depot about 1919, replacing the earlier wood station. The company's freight trains also transported coal from Pennsylvania to Cayuga Lake.

John Wilkinson is believed to be the individual standing on the wagon in this 1937 image taken on his northeast Ithaca farm. Many of the early local farmers produced grain, which could be processed at several Ithaca mills. Over time, farmers like the Wilkinsons adopted machinery such as the thresher photographed here.

The John Wilkinson farm was one of several local farms on North Triphammer Road in northeast Ithaca, a future commercial district. Pictured with their horses and threshing machine in November 1937 are, in no particular order, Gordon Wilkinson, Charles Gibbs, and Morey and Carl Eaton.

Gordon Wilkinson, Clifford Lane, and Jack Lynch load grain bags from a thresher on the Wilkinson farm in November 1937. The Ray, Butler, and Cornell-Taylor family farms were located down the road. Grain-threshing machines reduced farm labor by replacing handheld flails.

Employees of the Ithaca Public Works Department are photographed in front of the IPW Department building on Adams Street on June 7, 1938. From left to right are (first row) Lewis Cavone, Karlton Taylor, James Dougherty, Eddie Backner, Floyd Smith, Raymond Ryerson, Ben Poole, Richard Pelto, Ray Traynor, Paul Kirtchgrabber, Augie Macali, Joseph Massicci, Frank Pelleccioni, and Harry Hamilton; (second row) Frank Thomas, Frank Torchia, Fred Barto, Angelo Michel, William Swansbrough, Dominic Campagna, John Yenei, Richard Bowlsby, Joseph Lynch, Louis Alby, James Jackson, John Beach, Arthur Bacon, George Parks, Eugene Di Primio, Andy Pesoli, Robert Schutt, and Rocky Condi; (third row) Angelo Turco, G. Ksenak, Howard King, Fred Thomas, Peck Thompson, Percy Rorick, Chuck Thompson, Jack Guidi, William Ryan, Americo Pasquine, August Alby, Lew Ciccione, William Teeter, Brune Priori, Allen Jones, Mickey Dougherty, Frank De Libero, Matt Gray, Walter Blake, Robert Taylor, Louis Cascciotti, Frank Alby, and Ogden Kerr. (Photograph by Gray.)

Women assemble gun parts in the Ithaca Gun Company factory on Lake Street. Their contribution to the local workforce was important during World War II, as noted on the sign at left that reads, "Visiting slows up production of war material." The building formerly housed the Fall Creek Hub and Spoke Factory.

The steep site on Gun Hill is evident in this staff portrait at the Ithaca Gun Company factory. Among those pictured in the back row are Joseph Fendrick, standing in a white apron to the right of the entrance, and George Pia, just to the left. The company, which was located above Fall Creek, became internationally famous for its firearms.

From left to right, machinists Ginny, Phyllis, Phyl, and Lois stand in front of a 1944 machine model at the Morse Chain Works. As wartime workers, they joined women across the country entering the workforce during World War II. The Morse Chain Company formerly manufactured bicycle chains and moved to Ithaca from Trumansburg in 1906.

The Ithaca Farmer's Market hums with activity on May 23, 1977, the opening day of market season. At that time, the pavilion was located near the Station Restaurant in Ithaca's West End. The market later moved to Steamboat Landing on the Cayuga Inlet. (Photograph by Raymond Pompilio.)

Four

CITY ON THE LAKE
CAYUGA LAKE AND THE INLET

Many of Ithaca's creeks flow into the Cayuga Inlet and then Cayuga Lake. The Inlet has also served as a well-used transportation route, and for many years, the area was known as the Rhine, one of Ithaca's early neighborhoods. As W. Glenn Norris related in 1951, the name was possibly coined by a Cornell crewmember rowing on the Inlet. Residents were known as Rhiners, canalers, and squatters; they gained a reputation as a rough lot, but in reality, many were victims of illness and poverty resulting from fluctuating seasonal employment. The Inlet was known for its polluted waters.

As a transportation hub, the Inlet provided convenient access for fishermen, merchants, and recreational boaters. The Cornell crew team, officially formed in 1873, used the Inlet and the lake for practice and racing. Steamboats used a landing on the Inlet's old channel. Sandbars were removed, and as early as 1827, lake boats could use the Inlet's port rather than Port Renwick.

The first steamboats were in service on Cayuga Lake by 1820, led by the *Enterprise*. As the industry grew, many steamboats, both large and small, traveled up and down the lake, carrying passengers and towing coal, timber, and other freight. Several ended their runs after shipboard fires.

Recreational boating on the lake featured sailboats and yachts. Boat racing was a popular pastime, with sailboats such as the *Orphan* winning many competitions. The lakeshore also became a tourist destination by the late 1800s, with the development of Renwick Park, now known as Stewart Park.

A canal boat, the *J.L. Mott Jr.,* sits at the Benjamin F. Taber Boat Yard near the Cayuga Inlet, while boat yard workers and onlookers admire the vessel. The boat, which had been under construction, was soon to be launched. The Taber Boat Yard, which opened about 1850, produced many of Ithaca's boats until 1905. A variety of lake vessels was built there, including passenger steamboats and private steam yachts. The boat yard built Edward Wyckoff's yacht, the *Ezra Cornell,* and Charles Kellogg's private boat, the *Clara I.* Many boat yards were in business near Cayuga Lake and the Inlet in the middle to late 1800s. Often, sawmills accompanied the boat yards, where woodland trees along the lake were plentiful. The wood was then used to build steamboats, canal boats like that shown here, and other vessels for local residents and businesses.

Passengers on the steamboat *Kate Morgan* wait while the boat sits at the dock on a sunny day. The *Kate Morgan* was a passenger steamboat built at the Taber Boat Yard in 1850 and was owned in part by Timothy Dwight Wilcox, who was similarly invested in the other large steamboats. He bought the Cayuga Lake Steamboat Company in 1842.

The famous steamboat called the *Frontenac*, built in 1870 at the Taber Boat Yard, sits at the dock in this photograph, which was signed by the photographer in 1907. Until the early 1900s, the steamboat business flourished in Ithaca, taking locals and tourists up the lake. Several of the boats, most notably the *Frontenac* in 1907, ended their runs in tragedy, with fires aboard the wood vessels. (Photograph by J.A. Ricketts.)

Passengers wave from the deck of the Cayuga Lake steamboat named the *Mohawk*, which was in service from about 1901 to 1918. The boat's captain was Howard Brown, whose brother Clarence and father, Melvin T. Brown, were also steamboat captains around the turn of the century. The *Mohawk*, and the *Iroquois*, which was captained by Clarence, were small compared to Melvin's boat, the *Frontenac*.

The excursion boat *Helen* motors through Cayuga Lake waters. Recreational boating on the lake began in earnest about 1900, when boats with one or two cylinder motors were available for purchase. The 45-star American flag dates this photograph between 1896 and 1907, when Oklahoma became the 46th state.

The Jarvis Boat Yard owned this and other sailboats, which the business rented for use on Cayuga Lake. As early as 1875, there was also the William Jarvis Boat Livery, located on Cascadilla Creek. Sailboat competitions on the lake began in 1847 and ended during the Civil War but became popular again in the 1870s.

Renwick Pier and the steamboat landing are shown in this photograph taken from Renwick Beach on August 13, 1897. An earlier steamboat landing was located on the old channel of the Cayuga Inlet, which served as a public highway of sorts, beginning in 1821. The Inlet was used for both commercial and pleasure boating until 1894, when Renwick Park provided a dock for passenger boats.

Local residents and out-of-town visitors take advantage of mild weather at Renwick (later Stewart) Park on Cayuga Lake. Steamboat Pier, with its excursion and private boats, can be seen in the background in this 1890s image, while canoes wait at the shore. Financier Horace E. Hand and electrical engineer Herman Bergholtz bought the land at the south end of the lake by 1894. Naming the site after the original owner, they constructed Renwick Park as an amusement park with woods paths, a zoological garden, a beach, and a landing with rental passenger boats. The popular park also offered a vaudeville theater and concert pavilion. Thousands of visitors traveled from other areas to visit the park each summer. The name of the park was later changed to Stewart Park for Mayor Edwin C. Stewart, son of Ithaca's last president and first mayor, David Barnes Stewart.

Renwick Park continued for many years as a popular destination for locals and nonlocals alike. In these scenes captured about 1905, a band plays under the pagoda, and the Steamboat Pier can be seen. At that time, women often carried parasols on sunny days. The band, led by the well-known Pat Conway, performed at the park for many summers. Renwick Park's heyday began in the late 1800s and continued into the next century, as shown here by the crowds of visitors and the congestion of horse-drawn conveyances. The park was formed on property originally bought by James Renwick in 1790. His great-grandson James Jeffrey Renwick became the first superintendent of the park's gardens.

Humble dwellings like these along the Cayuga Inlet were common to the area known at the time as the Rhine. In this image captured around 1905, a man sits on a small dock just below the bank, while the houses on West Hill can be seen in the distance.

Two women stand with their dog on a bridge spanning the Inlet in this c. 1900 image. The buildings in the background are likely boathouses, used by Cayuga Lake fishermen and other boaters. In the early days of Ithaca's settlement, merchants often traveled by rowboats, such as that shown here, to transport wares.

This part of Cascadilla Creek was called "Shantytown" by locals. It was in the area of the Johnson Boatyard, across from the steamboat landing. This area was also known as Cascadilla Cove. Boathouses of Cayuga Lake fishermen were on the northern bank of the creek. Cayuga Inlet met Cascadilla Creek at this site.

The dredge boat *Ithaca* is shown in wintry waters. It was built at the Cayuga Inlet, where most local boats were constructed and painted. After 1911, when the Inlet became part of the Seneca Barge Canal Division, the state became responsible for dredging the Inlet.

Aviator Frank Burnside is depicted on this postcard at Cayuga Lake preparing to deliver mail by airplane. He was Tompkins County's first pilot, arriving in the area with the Thomas brothers of the Thomas Aeroplane Company. The company later merged with the Morse Chain Company in 1914. Burnside trained other pilots, including Paul Wilson of Ithaca, who became test pilots for the company.

The Thomas Brothers' hydroaeroplane on Cayuga Lake is featured in this postcard image. The plane was one of several tested by pilots on the lake. Cayuga Lake became a center of aviation when the company built two wooden hangars on the shore. By 1915, their hydroaeroplane was being flown on the lake by Thomas Flying School students.

The *Orphan* was purchased in 1901 by Claude H. Smith of the Ithaca Gun Company. George Houghton, businessman and sailor, was later the unofficial captain of the sailboat. The boat was eventually owned by four members of the Phi Kappa Sigma fraternity, who were also members of an orchestra called Paul Whiteman's Collegians. Finally, the *Orphan* found a home in the Great Lakes area, where one of its owners had a cottage.

Owned by Art Brown, the motorboat *Jean,* shown here, won the first race of the Ithaca Motor Boat Club on Cayuga Lake. The race began at Glenwood, went to McKinneys, then Tarbells, and returned to Glenwood. The boat completed the race in 26 minutes and 30 seconds. Later, Brown sold his boat to Charles McKinney. In 1923, the club's name changed to the Ithaca Yacht Club.

A crew team practices on the Cayuga Inlet, near the Seneca Street bridge. The first Cornell University rowers competed with a Springport (now Union Springs) team in 1872. The buildings at left were owned by the Delaware, Lackawanna and Western coal operations. The railroad transported coal north to Ithaca, where it was transferred to barges.

Rowers pass Johnson's Boat Yard in this 1942 image. The Cornell University crew team began intercollegiate racing in 1873. Fred E. Johnson's boat yard started in 1908 as a boat livery and later rented boats. Boat storage and a retail store followed. Although Johnson died in 1943, the business continues today.

Five

A COLLEGE TOWN
CORNELL UNIVERSITY AND ITHACA COLLEGE

Cornell University and Ithaca College have continued to grow in size, influence, and national prominence since their founding. Cornell was established in 1865 by Ezra Cornell and Andrew D. White and opened in 1868. Ezra Cornell, a former mill mechanic and farmer, became affluent through the national telegraph industry. White, a history professor, also valued scientific knowledge in that time of invention and evolving technology. The two men sought to create a university that would advance science but also provide a practical education in agriculture, mechanics, and manual labor for young men. Cornell also aimed to provide education for women within the university. Cornell University's first three stone buildings, known as Stone Row, were completed by 1869. By 1875, Sage College had opened within the university, admitting female students. The campus, its faculty, and student enrollment continued to grow.

The Ithaca Conservatory of Music, the precursor to Ithaca College, was founded in 1892 by professional violinist William Grant Egbert. His goal was to open a music school of the highest quality, and today Ithaca College continues to hold a strong national reputation for its music department. The Conservatory also sought to provide well-rounded higher education and opened the Affiliated Schools, which offered instruction in theater, physical education, and other subjects. The Ithaca Conservatory of Music became Ithaca College in 1931, and its South Hill campus opened in 1961. For a few years, some buildings, including the television-radio and speech-drama departments, remained downtown, while science classes were held at the Quarry Street campus. Today, Cornell University and Ithaca College are part of the fabric of Ithaca, with expanding campuses and ongoing involvement in the life of the community.

Four generations of Cornells sit for a family portrait. Pictured from left to right, youngest to oldest, are Charles Ezra, Alonzo, Ezra, and Elijah. At the time, young boys were often clothed in dresses. Ezra Cornell, originally pronounced "Corn'll," was born in 1807 at Westchester Landing, New York, in the Bronx borough of New York City. His father Elijah, a potter, bought a farm and moved the family in 1818 to DeRuyter, where Ezra helped build their log cabin. Many years later, Alonzo joined his father, Ezra, along with Andrew D. White and trustee Francis Miles Finch, in selecting the site for Cornell University's first buildings. After the institution was formally created on paper in 1865, the four men drove by horse and carriage to the future hilltop site of Morrill Hall. Despite arguments about the roadless and rough site far from the village below, Ezra prevailed and the men placed stakes for the first campus building.

At age 19, Ezra Cornell left his family's farm to work as a carpenter in Syracuse and Homer. In 1828, he walked the 43 miles from DeRuyter to Ithaca, where he continued his trade. He later became a mill mechanic. Ezra became known as Plaster Cornell for his work as the manager of Jeremiah S. Beebe's plaster and flour mills at Ithaca Falls. In 1831, he married Mary Ann Wood, the daughter of an Etna farmer. Over the years, Ezra continued working in carpentry and mills, and dabbled in real estate and groceries, later going back to farming. He left Ithaca for a time, engineered and built telegraph systems in many states and Quebec, founded the New York and Western Union Telegraph Company, and acquired his fortune. When he returned to Ithaca, Ezra bought a farm and raised vegetable crops and cattle. In 1861, he was elected as a state assemblyman, and two years later, state senator. Shortly thereafter, he founded Cornell University with Andrew D. White.

Born in Homer, New York, in 1832, Andrew D. White came from a wealthy family. At age seven he moved with his family to Syracuse. In 1849, he spent one year in the sophomore class at Geneva College, which eventually became Hobart College. He later went on to be a student at Yale University, graduating in 1853, and also studied history in France and Germany. In 1857, White accepted a professorship in history at the young University of Michigan and married Mary Outwater of Syracuse. In Michigan, White became an engaging and admired instructor. After returning to New York, he was elected to the state senate in 1863, at the same time as Ezra Cornell. The two men collaborated in founding Cornell University, and White became the new university's first president, serving until 1885. One of White's former University of Michigan students, Charles Kendall Adams, succeeded White as Cornell University president.

The founders and early faculty of Cornell University are pictured here in an 1869 composite portrait. Seated in the president's chair at left is Ezra Cornell and at right is Andrew D. White. The elaborate chair shown had been White's gift to the university and was reserved for special occasions. The university had just opened a year earlier. The first two faculty members were Evan W. Evans from Ohio, who began Cornell's mathematics department, and William Channing Russell, who taught history and modern languages. Louis Agassiz was a zoologist from Switzerland. In addition to serving as the university's librarian, Daniel Willard Fiske, a childhood friend of White, was a professor of northern European languages and director of the university press. Theodore W. Dwight from Columbia University taught constitutional law. British-born Goldwin Smith had been a professor of history at Oxford University and taught English history at Cornell. James Russell Lowell was a professor of English literature. (Photograph by Purdy and Frear.)

Early Cornell University students can be seen near Morrill Hall (left) in this c. 1873 photograph. Called Stone Row, Morrill, McGraw, and White Halls were the first university buildings, completed by 1869. The university opened in 1868. Built on Ezra Cornell's farmland, which was originally owned by Simeon DeWitt, the structures were designed by Archimedes Russell.

Cornell students walk through the snow near Sage College. Henry William Sage gave $250,000 to build the college, offering women the same educational provisions afforded to men. The cornerstone was placed on May 15, 1873. Henry Sage asserted at the time that, with his college, Cornell became the first university in the country to provide equal facilities for men and women.

By 1880, the Cornell University faculty had grown substantially. Andrew D. White was president and is believed to be seated in the second row, third from right. The elderly, white-bearded man to his right was Charles Chauncy Shackford, one of the university's first literature professors.

Liberty Hyde Bailey, far right, became professor of horticulture at Cornell University in 1888. He is remembered as one of the university's best teachers. He was a prolific science writer who also produced books of poetry, and was a founder of the nature study movement, known today as environmental education. Cornell University's L.H. Bailey Hortorium Herbarium houses one of the largest collections of preserved plants, and was founded by Bailey.

Photographed about 1891, Sage Chapel is shown before it underwent renovation and while McGraw Tower was still under construction. The chapel was designed by the Rev. Charles Babcock, who was the first professor of architecture at Cornell University and later became director of the Department of Architecture. Although Babcock was an Episcopal priest, the church was nonsectarian, one of the first of its kind in the country.

The strikingly elaborate interior of Sage Chapel on the Cornell campus was completed during the structure's renovation in 1903. The work in 1903 was one of four expansions that took place, the first three of which were supervised by church designer Charles Babcock. The original building was financed by university trustee Henry William Sage.

Cornell University students relax on the lawn near the University Library in this image from the late 1800s. A horse and carriage wait near McGraw Tower. Jennie McGraw donated the tower's bells and chimes in 1868. The library, which was designed by local architect William H. Miller, was dedicated in 1891. Before the library was constructed, the book collection had occupied a cramped space in Morrill Hall and later McGraw Hall on the Arts Quad.

Members of the Cornell University Bicycle Corps stand in formation on the Arts Quad in 1897. Bicycling as a sport began on campus by 1883. Public bicycling had become a traffic hazard on campus. That year, the executive committee began prohibiting bicycles on sidewalks; they also prohibited freely roaming animals, such as sheep, horses, and cows.

This view of the Cornell University campus photographed in 1901 shows the university's proximity to Cayuga Lake. At right are the three buildings that comprised Stone Row. Visible at left, near the lake, is the grand McGraw-Fiske mansion, designed by William H. Miller and built for heiress Jennie McGraw-Fiske. After her death, which took place before she was able to move into the home, the building became a fraternity. Her widower was university librarian D. Willard Fiske.

Class Day festivities take place at Cornell University in this June 1912 image. The site is likely the Library Slope, just below the central campus buildings. Graduates are pictured to the left and in the crowd, while families and other guests watch the proceedings from benches on the hill.

82

Goldwin Smith Hall is under construction in this c. 1904 image. A large wood structure had once occupied the site, containing agricultural, photographic, and chemical laboratories. A dairy husbandry center—the state's first gift to the university—had also been on the site. The center eventually became the site of the north wing of Goldwin Smith Hall.

Goldwin Smith Hall, the Hall of Humanities, stands behind Grecian columns and the statue of Andrew D. White along the Cornell University Arts Quad. Beyond is Lincoln Hall, then Sibley Hall, distinguished by a prominent dome that was completed by 1902. In 1906, Goldwin Smith Hall became the location of the Museum of Casts, housing ancient statuary assembled by Alfred Emerson, the university's first professor of archaeology and art.

TOBOGANNING

Cornell University students and other young people watch from the south edge of Beebe Lake as two tobogganers race down the campus run early in the 1900s. At the slide's 1902 opening, Cornell president Jacob Gould Schurman, Dean Thomas (T.F.) Crane, Prof. Johnny Parson, and a student climbed aboard a toboggan at the top of the run and launched toward the frozen lake at 48.6 mph. To pay for the slide's construction, students and other local visitors paid 5¢ per toboggan on Saturdays during the first winter. The frozen lake was also a popular skating area. Before 1917, the original wooden slide was replaced by one of steel, made locally by the Groton Bridge Company. The tobaggan run was a popular albeit dangerous recreation site throughout its tenure, until the 1939–1940 season, when 21 injuries spelled its demise.

84

Cornell students participate in a candle lighting ceremony at the College of Home Economics in this c. 1920s image. Professor Martha Van Rensselaer was instrumental in the creation of the college in 1925. Initially an instructor in the home economics department, Van Rensselaer had became involved in the Home Conservation Division of the US Food Administration and advocated for a new college to be formed within the university. (Photograph by John P. Troy.)

This aerial view of the Cornell campus dates from the 1920s, when Livingston Farrand was the university president (1921 to 1937). The vast, open countryside beyond campus is striking compared to today's view. Cornell Plantations was not yet established; work by the Civilian Conservation Corps began in 1935. (Photograph by John P. Troy.)

85

Rothschild Brothers was a popular and longstanding department store at 215 East State Street. The building was also the edifice of the Ithaca Conservatory of Music, as can be seen on the sign above the second-story windows. The school had originally opened in four rented rooms in the Day house on East Seneca Street and moved to the Wilgus Opera House in the Rothschild Building in 1894.

William Grant Egbert founded the Ithaca Conservatory of Music in 1892 and was musical director. With him on the steps of the Conservatory Building is student Helen Doyle Durrett, class of 1913. Born in Danby in 1867 and a violinist since childhood, Egbert was believed to have performed his first concert at age seven. He later studied at Syracuse University and in Germany. He was the conservatory's president until 1924.

The Ithaca
Conservatory of
Music purchased
the home of
Judge Douglass
Boardman at 120
East Buffalo Street
on November 1,
1910, to house
the school. The
mortgage price
was $11,400. The
building was
renovated and the
school moved from
the Rothschild
Building to the
Boardman House
in time for the
1911 school year.

The Ithaca Conservatory of Music Concert Hall, later called the Little Theatre, is pictured to the left of the Conservatory Building on this postcard. Originally called Conservatory Hall, the Concert Hall was designed by New York City architects Cady and Gregory and included an auditorium, reception and reading rooms, studios and offices, and the Elocution Hall, later known as the Green Room. The building was completed by fall 1913.

The auditorium at Conservatory Hall is featured on this postcard from the Ithaca Conservatory of Music. Seats were removed for dancing and other classes on the lower level, and elaborate musical and dramatic productions were performed on the stage. A fraternal society called the Amards was in charge of presenting plays and recitals, the ticket sales from which were used to furnish the hall with costumes, draperies, and other materials.

Members of the Ithaca Conservatory of Music orchestra are pictured with their instruments in 1913. The school had just moved to its DeWitt Park location from the Rothschild Department Store building two years earlier. The school's popular dramatic and musical performances drew local audiences for many years.

Students and instructors stand for a 1920s portrait in front of the Ithaca School of Physical Education (ISPE) on East Seneca Street. Dr. Albert H. Sharpe became dean of the school in 1921. Part of the Ithaca Conservatory of Music, ISPE was one of the Affiliated Schools, formed to broaden the educational offerings available to Conservatory students.

In this 1951 image, the Seneca Gym has a prominent Ithaca College sign. The Catholic Youth Organization played their home games here in the 1950s. The college consolidated the Ithaca Conservatory of Music and the Affiliated Schools, such as the building's former occupant, ISPE. The building was formerly home to the Star Theatre. (Photograph by C. Hadley Smith.)

Members of the Sigma Alpha Iota sorority are pictured on the front porch of their Ithaca College sorority house at 440 East Buffalo Street. The sorority was formed before the Ithaca Conservatory of Music became Ithaca College in 1931. Representatives from several sororities and other student groups were already serving on the Conservatory's student council by 1920. The Women's Self Government Association was also active.

The downtown Ithaca College campus included, from left to right, the Little Theatre, Boardman Hall, and the radio-television building on East Buffalo Street, in addition to other buildings. The first course in radio was offered in 1931. The college's radio programs were first broadcast on Elmira's WESG station in 1933. The building at right was constructed in 1954 and was originally used as the college library. In 1958, a second-floor television and radio facility was unveiled.

The fourth president of Ithaca College, Dr. Howard I. Dillingham, left, is shown with a scale model of a new building planned for the college's South Hill campus. Dillingham served as president of the college from 1957 until 1970. He succeeded Leonard B. Job, who held the office from 1932 until 1957. Dillingham was born in 1904 in Elba, New York, and studied at the University of Pennsylvania, and later at Syracuse University, where he earned a PhD in education and was employed in the 1930s. He then became dean of Rider College and was a school headmaster. Before Dillingham became president of Ithaca College, he was assistant to the president from 1951 to 1953 and then vice president. The college moved from multiple downtown locations to a new South Hill campus during the early years of Dillingham's presidency.

By 1968, when this photograph was taken, Ithaca College's South Hill campus had been growing for eight years. The college's spectacular view of Cayuga Lake can be seen in the background. One of the two Tower Dormitories stands just to the right of the Caroline Werner Gannett Center. (Photograph by C. Hadley Smith.)

This aerial view of the Ithaca College campus on South Hill was taken in 1971. At the lower left, Route 96 extends from South Aurora Street. At that time, Ellis L. Phillips Jr. was president of the college, serving from 1970 until 1975. Like many colleges at the time, Ithaca campus life became turbulent during the 1960s but by 1971 student protests diminished. (Photograph by C. Hadley Smith.)

Six

ITHACA FIRSTS
ITHACA'S CLAIMS TO FAME

Although Ithaca is well known for its educational institutions, the community has had other claims to fame, some lighthearted and others more dignified. One of the best known is Ithaca's creation of the first ice cream sundae. Ithaca is not the only city to lay claim to the invention, but according to local lore, and backed by historical documentation, the Platt and Colt Pharmacy created the "Cherry Sunday" at their soda fountain, as advertised in the *Ithaca Journal* in 1892.

Ithaca is also one of a handful of cities historically known for having polydactyl cats, that is, cats with an unusual number of toes. One of these felines, named Caesar Grimalkin, was the model for a nationally famous toy first produced in the 1890s. The Ithaca Kitty, as it came to be known, was one of the earliest stuffed toys to be manufactured.

Ithaca's telephone service was among the country's earliest, but the movie industry may be one of the city's most famous, though fleeting, historical chapters. In 1913, the Wharton brothers began producing silent films in Ithaca. The following year, they founded Wharton Studios. Several of their movies were filmed here, using both natural areas and city buildings in many scenes. Local residents were often recruited as extras, and famous actors, including Lionel Barrymore, came to town. The studio's last Ithaca film was a 1919 or 1920 production.

Many of Ithaca's other industries gained fame beyond the Finger Lakes region. Among them was the Thomas-Morse Aircraft Corporation. Ithaca has also had its share of notable visitors, including several former presidents and icons such as pilot Amelia Earhart.

Caesar Grimalkin, a tiger cat with seven toes on each front paw, belonged to the family of Celia and William Hazlitt Smith and their daughter Madge. Grimalkin and the Smiths shared a home at 116 Oak Avenue. In 1890, Celia and her sister-in-law, Charity Smith, created one of the country's first stuffed toys for Madge, and they used Caesar as their model. When the toy was mass-produced, Caesar became Ithaca's first famous feline. (Photograph by Charles H. Howes.)

DESIGN.

C. M. SMITH.
STATUETTE.

No. 21,680.   Patented July 5, 1892.

The Smiths applied for a patent on the Ithaca Kitty toy in 1892, and from its first printing as a fabric pattern, the sew-at-home toy became widely popular in the United States and London. It was exhibited at the 1893 World's Columbian Exposition in Chicago. Nearly 200,000 sold in the first holiday season. The first Ithaca shop to sell the toy prints was Andrus and Church on East State Street.

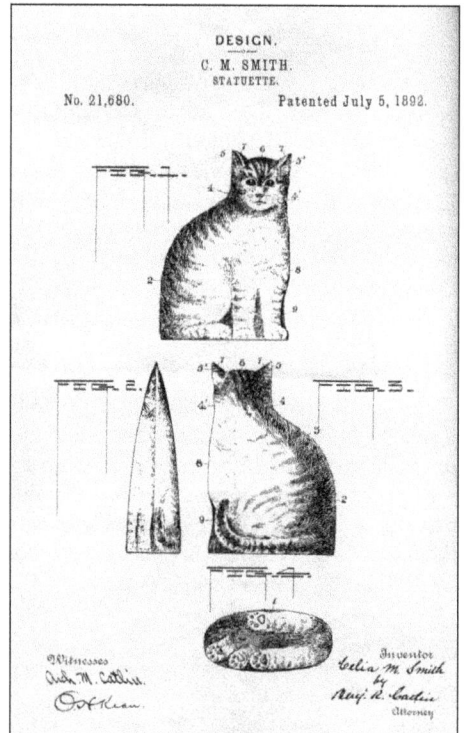

Theodore Roosevelt, in the foreground on horseback, visits the City Cemetery on University Avenue around 1900. This photograph may have been taken during Roosevelt's 1899 visit to Cornell University, when he was governor of New York state. He also traveled to the area when he spoke in Newfield in 1910, soon after he completed his presidential term in 1909.

The 30-foot dam on Six Mile Creek, completed in 1903, was the first dome dam ever built. Civil engineer and Cornell University professor Gardner Stewart Williams designed a 90-foot dam, but he had to revise his plan at the request of the Ithaca Water Works Company. The dam created a reservoir from which water was routed through iron pipes to the Purification Works. The creek still provides the city's water supply today.

On October 8, 1909, the Honorary Commercial Commissioners from Japan arrived in Ithaca. They visited the Cornell University campus and paraded through the city via motorcade. Ithaca was the smallest of the 69 American cities visited by the commissioners and their wives. The purpose of their trip was to allow Japan and the United States to become more acquainted after many years of Japan's restrictions against foreign visitors. The dignitaries included several professors and officials from Japan. The local Congregational church minister William Eliot Griffis had visited Japan in 1867 and became Ithaca's expert on the country. He prepared a letter-to-the editor of the newspaper that included recommendations on how best to welcome the Japanese entourage.

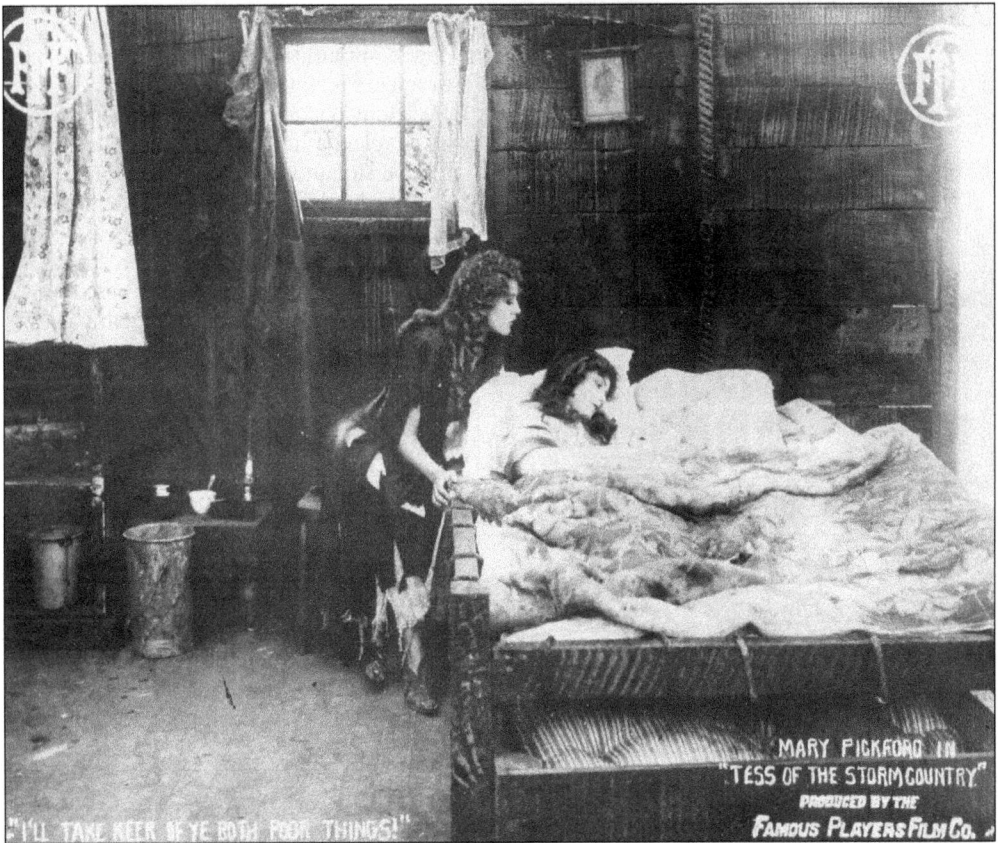

"I'LL TAKE KEER OF YE BOTH POOR THINGS!"

MARY PICKFORD IN
"TESS OF THE STORM COUNTRY"
PRODUCED BY THE
FAMOUS PLAYERS FILM Co.

Mary Pickford starred in the silent film *Tess of the Storm Country,* which was set in the Rhine neighborhood although not filmed in Ithaca. A mother and baby rest inside a humble cabin, while the subtitle for this scene reads, "I'll take keer of ye both poor things!" Produced by the Famous Players Film Company, the movie was based on Grace Miller White's 1909 novel.

Originally from Cortland, songwriter William Dillon lived in Ithaca for many years. Born in 1878, he grew up in a musical and theatrical family. Dillon became a vaudeville performer and songwriter. A song he wrote in 1911, *I Want a Girl Just Like the Girl that Married Dear Old Dad,* sold more than five million copies of recordings and sheet music. It was recorded by Harry Von Tilzer.

In 1878, Ithaca was one of the country's first communities to have telephone service. Previously, Prof. William Anthony had connected two telephones via a telegraph line, between Cornell University and his College Avenue home. The Federal Telephone and Telegraph Company building shown here was completed about 1912 on North Tioga Street. The company was purchased by the New York Telephone Company in 1921, and the telephone systems merged.

Creighton Hale, Lionel Barrymore, and Pearl White are shown in a scene from *The Romance of Elaine.* This serial movie was filmed in Ithaca in 1916. Barrymore's role was a villain named Marcus del Marr, but he left before finishing the film. Leopold and Theodore Wharton produced silent films at Renwick Park, using Ithaca, known as the Hollywood of the East, as the setting for several movies between about 1913 and 1920.

The Wharton Studios silent movie *Patria* included scenes filmed using this miniature village as a backdrop, complete with a company store and a boat. Here, the set designers, with tools in hand, pose with their handiwork. The serial film was produced during World War I, before the United States joined forces. *Patria* was a patriotic propaganda film.

Actors Irene Castle and Milton Sills perform a scene for the silent film *Patria* in 1916. Behind them stand actors Warner Oland and George Majeroni, just outside Goldwin Smith Hall on the Cornell University campus. The film was a 15-episode serial. Castle lived in Ithaca and was briefly married to Robert Elias Treman.

In this film still from the Wharton Studios 1918 production *The Eagle's Eye*, actresses appear above the caption, "Dixie Mason, of the Secret Service, joins the female division of the I.W.W." Locals were often recruited as extras, but the studio also brought many notable actors to town for their films.

The subtitle for this film still from *The Eagle's Eye* reads, "Mrs. Blank scorns Von Bernstorff and spurns his bride." The film was the last of the Wharton brothers' Ithaca serials. It included a reenactment of the sinking of the *Lusitania*, filmed at Cayuga Lake. Other Ithaca locations used included an iced-over Beebe Lake and the Methodist church. Wharton Studios later moved to the warmer climate of California.

Arthur Buckingham, right, works on an airplane wing about 1921. The Thomas-Morse Aircraft Corporation had manufactured the famous Thomas-Morse Scout, or Tommy Scout, planes in Ithaca in 1917–1918 for the United States military. The company also built many other types of airplanes over the years. The business was later bought by Bell Aircraft Company.

Louis Agassiz Fuertes was an internationally acclaimed artist whose favorite subjects were birds. Called the father of modern bird art, Fuertes was born in 1874 and graduated from Cornell University in 1897. After his death in 1927, the Fuertes Bird Sanctuary was established in Stewart Park, and many of his paintings are still on exhibit today at the Cornell Lab of Ornithology.

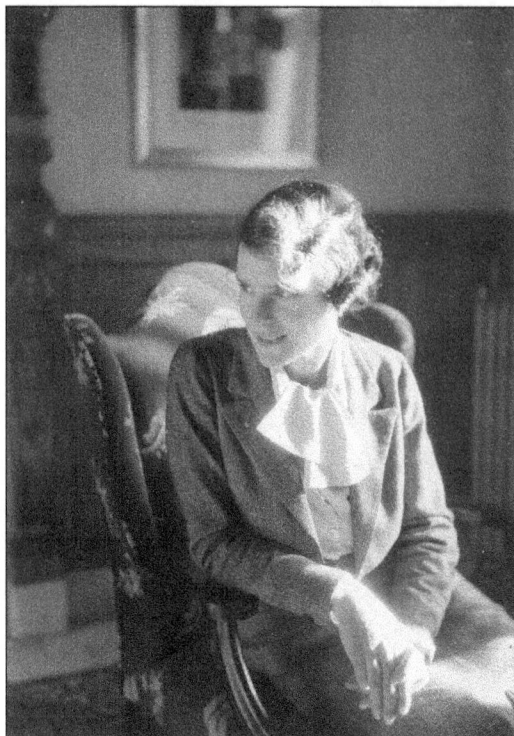

Margaret Bourke-White was born in 1904 in New York City. She studied at Cornell University and worked for local photographer Henry Head. She became a nationally known photographer for *Time* and *Fortune* magazines in the 1930s. In 1936, she was hired at *Life* magazine and worked there for many years. Much of her work as a photojournalist focused on architectural and industrial images. (Photograph by Henry Head.)

Famous pilot Amelia Earhart pays a visit to Ithaca. Here, she stands before an airplane wing at the old Ithaca airport on Taughannock Boulevard, which was later converted into the Hangar Theatre. Standing to Earhart's immediate right is John E. Hoffman, who worked for Robinson Serial Surveys in the late 1930s. He provided five-minute flights over Cayuga Lake.

Playbills from the Strand Theatre feature the names Katharine Hepburn and Mae West. Hepburn played Tracy Lord in *The Philadelphia Story*, and West starred in the 1946 play *Come On Up*. The Strand Theatre was built in 1917 at 310–312 East State Street for traveling professional theater groups. It was also used as a movie theater. Other notable visiting actors and vaudeville performers who visited the Strand included George M. Cohan, Katherine Cornell, Dorothy Gish, Helen Hayes, and Erich von Stroheim. The theater accommodated large audiences, with 1,600 seats. In the 1950s, television and film had replaced theatre in popularity and the Strand Theatre was used exclusively for movies.

STRAND
THEATRE

The Theatre Guild, Inc.

Presents

The Philadelphia Story

A new comedy by PHILIP BARRY

with

KATHARINE HEPBURN

Van Heflin   Joseph Cotten   Nicholas Joy

Directed by ROBERT B. SINCLAIR

Designed and Lighted by ROBERT EDMOND JONES

Production under the supervision of
THERESA HELBURN and LAWRENCE LANGNER

CAST

DINAH LORD	Played by	Lenore Lonergan
MARGARET LORD	"	Viola Roache
TRACY LORD	"	KATHARINE HEPBURN
ALEXANDER LORD	"	Dan Tobin
THOMAS	"	Owen Coll
WILLIAM TRACY	"	Forrest Orr
ELIZABETH IMBRIE	"	Ruth Holden
MACAULAY CONNOR	"	Van Heflin
GEORGE KITTREDGE	"	Frank Fenton
C. K. DEXTER HAVEN	"	Joseph Cotten
EDWARD	"	Philip Foster
SETH LORD	"	Nicholas Joy
MAY	"	Dora Sayers
ELSIE	"	Hope Buckeley
MAC	"	Brent Sargent

STRAND
THEATRE

THURSDAY, OCTOBER 31, 1946

◆

SELECT OPERATING CORPORATION

presents

MAE WEST

in

"COME ON UP"

A New Comedy by

Miles Mander, Fred Schiller and Thomas Dunphy

◆

Directed by Russell Fillmore—Setting by Ernest Glover

◆

Costumes furnished by
STAGE COSTUMES, INC.
3 W. 61st St., New York City

Former president Harry S. Truman stands in front of a Mohawk Airlines plane in Ithaca on April 18, 1960. Escorted by a secret service agent, Truman arrived in Ithaca and visited Cornell University later that day. At Barton Hall, filled with 9,000 people, he presented a lecture titled, "The American President." The Student Government Executive Board had invited him to speak at the university. (Photograph by C. Hadley Smith.)

Former president Dwight D. Eisenhower, right, visited Ithaca on May 17, 1963. Here, he walks with Cornell University president Deane Waldo Mallott and his wife, Eleanor, at the Ithaca airport. The leaders were longtime friends, having met as youths in Abilene, Kansas. Mallott hosted a lunch at the A.D. White House for Eisenhower, who later spoke for 15 minutes to 6,000 people in Barton Hall. (Photograph by C. Hadley Smith.)

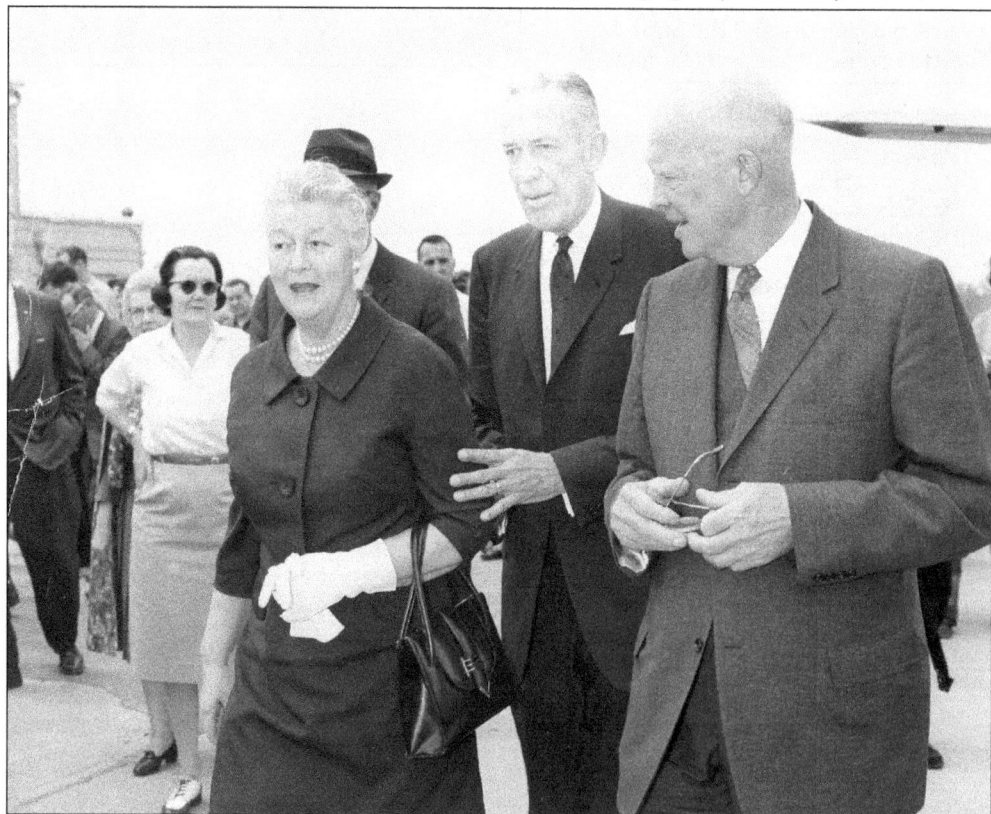

Seven

AN ENLIGHTENED CITY
COMMUNITY INVOLVEMENT

Today Ithaca is known by many as a progressive and forward-thinking city, with residents involved in social justice work, environmental issues, and community organizing. Community-minded citizens lead neighborhood associations, volunteer for nonprofit organizations, or start their own. Others serve on city and town boards and committees, attend municipal meetings, and voice their opinions on important issues.

This idealism and involvement has been part of Ithaca since before the area had a formal name. The first town meeting, when the area was still part of the town of Ulysses, is believed to have taken place on April 7, 1795, at the cabin of Peter Hinepaw. The first village election was held on May 8, 1821, in Jesse Grant's Coffee House, a tavern at 8–14 (now 106–112) East State Street.

Early Ithacans were involved in a number of important issues. George A. Johnson, a local barber, became a pivotal leader in the Underground Railroad. Elizabeth Beebe worked diligently to aid the ill and poor residents of the Inlet area, despite her own failing health.

The Southside Community Center, dedicated in 1938, was built collaboratively by local residents and the federal Works Progress Administration. Director James L. Gibbs led the center, which offered programs for young and old. He is honored today with a street named after him near the Ithaca Youth Bureau. In addition to Southside activities, children became involved in the community through scouting, park cleanup events such as Community Day in 1917, and parades.

Ithaca's parades have played an important role in civic spirit, from honoring volunteer firemen, unions, and other local organizations, to celebrating the community at the annual Ithaca Festival. Celebration has long been part of Ithaca's history.

Following a legislative act, Ithaca's first election was held in 1821. Chosen as trustees were Daniel Bates, Andrew DeWitt Bruyn, Julius Ackley, William R. Collins, and George Blythe. They elected Bates as president of the board and of the village of Ithaca for one year. Andrew DeWitt Bruyn, pictured here, was the second president of the village of Ithaca, elected in 1822. He was born about 1791 and grew up in the Hudson Valley. With the encouragement of his cousin, Ithaca's Simeon DeWitt, Bruyn moved to Ithaca in 1812. Five years later, he built a house at the northwest corner of Cayuga and Buffalo Streets. Before becoming president of Ithaca, he held a number of local offices, including commissioner of Ithaca schools. He was elected supervisor of the town and village in 1825 and later became a United States congressman. (Photograph by Ellsworth McGillivray.)

The St. James African Methodist Episcopal Zion Church at 116 Wheat Street (now Cleveland Avenue) is shown in this early photograph, taken between 1898 and 1904. The congregation first organized in 1833, and it was a center of the African American community. It formed when congregation members left the segregated Methodist Episcopal church on Aurora Street to form their own church. Harriet Tubman was one of its early visitors, and it is believed that Frederick Douglass also visited. The church was active in the abolitionist movement and was an important stop on the Underground Railroad, providing shelter to many former slaves. While over time, the church has been renovated and enlarged, St. James is the oldest church building in Ithaca. (Photograph by Seth L. Sheldon.)

George A. Johnson was born in 1835 and later lived on South Cayuga Street. In Ithaca, he was a prominent local citizen and a well-known barber with a business on State Street. He was actively involved in the Underground Railroad in Ithaca, helping 114 slaves gain their freedom. At times, he collaborated with his friend and Ithaca attorney Ben Johnson, who in 1825 had been the fourth president of the village, in providing safe passage for escaped slaves heading to Canada from the South. Ben provided provisions and transportation on a Cayuga Lake steamboat. The local Underground Railroad network was most active during the 1840s and after 1850, when the Fugitive Slave Act was passed. From 1872 to 1873, George A. Johnson served as doorkeeper for the New York State Senate. He died in 1919. This portrait was taken between about 1910 and 1912. (Photograph by Ellsworth McGillivray.)

Hayt's Chapel was built on land given by Deacon Charles Hayt in the 1850s. A schoolhouse and cemetery were located next to the church. The chapel was erected at Hayts Corners on Ithaca's West Hill as a place of worship for a small group of Christians representing a variety of denominations. The congregation was active in the local abolitionist movement.

Elizabeth Beebe was an Ithaca resident who was called "the city missionary." Several churches collaborated on building the Inlet Mission on Cliff Street, where Beebe led chapel services. She served the Inlet, or Rhine, community, using donations from churches and individuals. Born in 1843 in Canada, she administered to the sick and poor residents of the Inlet until her death in 1905. She stood for this portrait in 1864.

Jane McGraw planned and commissioned a home for elderly women. The Home was completed in 1877 at the corner of South Aurora Street and Hillview Place. The building was later given to the Ladies Union Benevolent Society to serve Ithaca's needy residents. A new facility to replace the Home was built for retired residents in the early 1970s on South Geneva Street and named McGraw House.

This parade was held in October 1880 on East State Street. The parade of the Knights Templar Conclave of New York State, a temperance organization, also featured Winfield Scott Hancock, a Democratic nominee for United States president. Visible at right is Mrs. A. Boys' millinery and 99¢ store at 51 East State Street.

110

Ithaca president Daniel W. Burdick and the village board of trustees pose for a portrait about 1887. Burdick was the 43rd president, serving from March 1887 to March 1888. At the beginning of his term, the trustees chose 16 citizens to draw up a charter, changing the village to a city. The charter became a law on May 2, 1887, and took effect the following year.

Ithacans watch a parade along Tioga Street at the corner of State Street in this c. 1900 image. The Corner Book Store, in the Finch Block at 158 East State Street, is shown at right, while a trolley car destined for Stewart Avenue can be seen on State Street. The bookstore opened in the 1830s at another location and was later moved to this site, where it remained until 1923.

The city of Ithaca's Common Council formed in 1888 under the city's first mayor, David Barnes Stewart. He is seated third from right, while clerk Charles A. Ives leans at the table, pen in hand. On June 1, 1888, the city charter took effect, and Ithaca made the transition from village to city. The president became mayor, and the Board of Trustees became the Common Council. Mayors were elected for two-year terms and were given the authority to appoint many city officials. The event was celebrated by local officials and guests in a dignified ceremony, which was presided over by Mayor Stewart.

The 44th and last president of Ithaca was chosen in a contentious election. David Barnes Stewart had grown up on a Newfield farm and went into business in cigars, groceries, and commercial real estate. Elected by 328 votes, he defeated Collingwood Bruce Brown, who had been president in 1886 and 1887. At the time, political conflicts were rampant. With street paving and sewer system projects, and new government commissions with paid officials, the cost to the local government was reportedly over $1 million. Government spending, political maneuvering by party leaders, and disagreement over the appointment of the police justice were some of the issues at hand. As the last president, Stewart also became the first mayor of Ithaca. The Common Council later changed the name of Factory Street to Stewart Avenue in honor of the first mayor, who was known as a progressive leader who served the city without a salary.

The International Alliance of Theatrical Stage Employees (IATSE) participated with a float in a downtown parade around 1900 on State Street. The group included the stagehands' union of the Lyceum Theater. It had been in business at 113 South Cayuga Street since 1893, and was known as a grand theater. The Lyceum closed after about 30 years.

The Central New York Fireman's Convention was held in Ithaca in 1894. The convention's parade on August 9 was a well-attended community event, at which the city welcomed the firemen with banners and flags. The parade route on Cayuga Street is crossing State Street in this image. One banner reads "Cayuga Hose," a longtime local fire company.

On September 12, 1907, Ithaca held a volunteer firemen's parade. Here, members of the Protective Fire Police, Company Eight, are shown in their marching attire. Capt. Roger B. Williams led the group in the parade as they marched on Cayuga Street. Eight fire departments participated in the event.

Members of the Ithaca Common Council are shown in this 1916 portrait. The role of the council members included proposing ordinances and approving mayoral appointments of city officials. Frederick E. Bates served as mayor of the city in 1916 and 1917. He was succeeded by Frank B. Davis, who served in 1918 and 1919.

The officers of Calvary Baptist Church stand for a portrait. Standing at center, next to the pulpit, is the Rev. Benjamin H. Payne. He became pastor in 1926 and served the congregation for 39 years. Until 1903, the church was named the Wesleyan ME, or Methodist Episcopal, and became an outgrowth of the St. James AME Zion Church in about 1857.

Members of the congregation at Calvary Baptist Church on North Albany Street sit for a c. 1926 photograph. Identified here on the right side of the congregation is Rev. Benjamin H. Payne in the fourth-row aisle seat, William Randolph in the first-row aisle seat, and on the left is Lydia Phillips Houchins in the second row, fourth from the left.

These photographs show Ithaca's first Community Day on May 15, 1917. Thousands of city residents walked to the Six Mile Glen Park to attend the park's opening in the creek gorge, which included the area below the Columbia Street bridge. In a real community spirit, many brought tools and improved trails, cleared debris, and plowed the children's gardens. Other areas included an amphitheater, a baseball field, a field for flag exercises, a playground, and woods. A gift to the city by Robert H. Treman, the park and its opening celebration were organized by the Bureau of Commerce to inspire civic pride. (Photographs by Seth L. Sheldon.)

Ithacans walk up the Six Mile Creek gorge from the bottom of East State Street during Community Day in 1917. High school students had built the park's footbridges, which community members improved during the celebration and workday. The park extended as far as the area below Van Natta's dam on Giles Street. Cornelia Williams, a teacher who lived just up the hill at 321 Columbia Street, had coordinated the planting of the school gardens with South Hill School students, below the Columbia Street bridge. Local women donated about 50 gallons of coffee and 2,000 sandwiches for the event. (Photographs by Seth L. Sheldon.)

Members of Boy Scout Troop 12, the troop from the Catholic church, pose here with their leader for a 1928 portrait. Shown from left to right are (first row) Louis Cornish, L. Terry, Robert Powers, Stan Gregg, Elmer Morgan, Walter Sullivan, Bill Morris, and Jim Clark; (second row) ? Bernardi, Lester Nemes, Mike Strok, Ed Barron, Matt Meiczinger, Bill Murphy, Mike Nemes, and E. Miller; (third row) John Bangs, Geo Hagin, John Whalen, Hugh Gibbs, Jim Driscoll, Bob McCormick, and Roger Keane; (fourth row) William Keane, Paul Goetchius, William McCann, Scout Master George Loveless, Ron Sheldon, Dick Messer, unidentified, and Joseph Fendrick. Ithaca's first Boy Scout troop, for boys age 12 and older, was formed in 1912, two years after scouting began nationally when the program was chartered by Congress. The local Boy Scout council was later named for bird artist Louis Agassiz Fuertes.

This advertisement was produced by the Paramount Publicity Corporation of New York City. It was shown on movie theater screens in Ithaca and was commissioned by the Ithaca Board of Commerce, similar to today's chamber of commerce. Even then, buying locally was considered important for Ithaca's economy, as well as for civic pride, as advertised here.

BUY WHERE YOU LIVE

"etter late than never."
Won't YOU get in line?

COME! It's no task whatever;
The water's fine!
JOIN THE BOOM FOR CIVIC PRIDE,
And make OUR town known
FAR AND WIDE.

CIVIC PRIDE

ITHACA BOARD OF COMMERCE
An Organization for Community Service

Participants in the Ithaca Pet Parade pose for a snapshot during the event, about 1932. The children have competition numbers pinned to their coats, while their dogs endure the spectacle. Standing at the far right is Jack Clynes. At center, standing to the left of the woman in an overcoat, are Lou Beardsley and A. Carver. The parade took place on Aurora Street.

Southside Community Center was built in part by the Works Progress Administration (WPA) and completed by 1938. The Francis Harper Woman's Club began fundraising in 1927 for an activities center for African American youth. In 1928, the Servus League was founded and Jessie Cooper served as president. A rental house at 221 South Plain Street was used as a community center. By 1930, the group's name changed to Southside Community Center, and the organization bought a house at 305 South Plain Street two years later. In 1936, a lot next door was purchased, the house torn down, and the new center was built with the help of the WPA and Ithaca's Common Council. (Photograph below by Dan Nero.)

First Lady Eleanor Roosevelt, left, looks on while holding a bouquet in her lap at the dedication ceremony for Southside Community Center. Standing at far right is Isaiah, or Ike, Murray, while Mayor Joseph Meyer stands behind the podium. The key to the center was presented to Murray. Mrs. Roosevelt dedicated the new activities center on February 17, 1938.

James A. Ross, left, director of racial relations for the Works Progress Administration of New York state, greets Alfred Edgar Smith, administrative assistant for the WPA in Washington, D.C. These officials were attending the Southside Community Center dedication ceremony in 1938. The construction project employed 14 workers.

James L. Gibbs looks on as Robert Treman signs the guest book at Southside Community Center. Between them is Treman's wife, Carolyn. Others in attendance include, from left to right, Beatrice Hemans, Anna Johnson, Evelyn Rucker, and Ora Spaulding, the widow of Levi Spaulding, Ithaca's first African-American policeman. Gibbs was a prominent community leader, director of the community center, and at one time was president of the local NAACP.

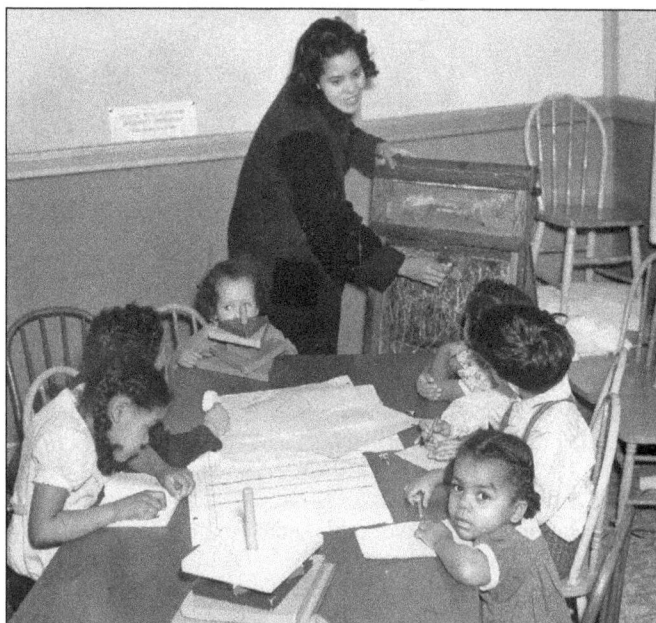

In March 1939, the Works Progress Administration again visited Southside Community Center to photograph and report on the center's progress in its first year. The Tot's Class was an after-school activity time for children of working mothers. The teacher was Mamie Andrews. The children in this photograph are, clockwise starting at left, Lilly Johnson, unidentified, Pattie John, two unidentified, and Anna Robbins facing the camera. (Photograph by Dan Nero.)

The WPA photographer captured this image of Girl Scout Troop 14 members during his March 1, 1939, visit to Southside Community Center. The color guard included, from left to right, Julia Broughton, Betty John, Lenora Bell, and Barbara Bell. They posed in the large second floor meeting room, where a variety of fraternal and recreational youth groups and adult groups gathered. (Photograph by Dan Nero.)

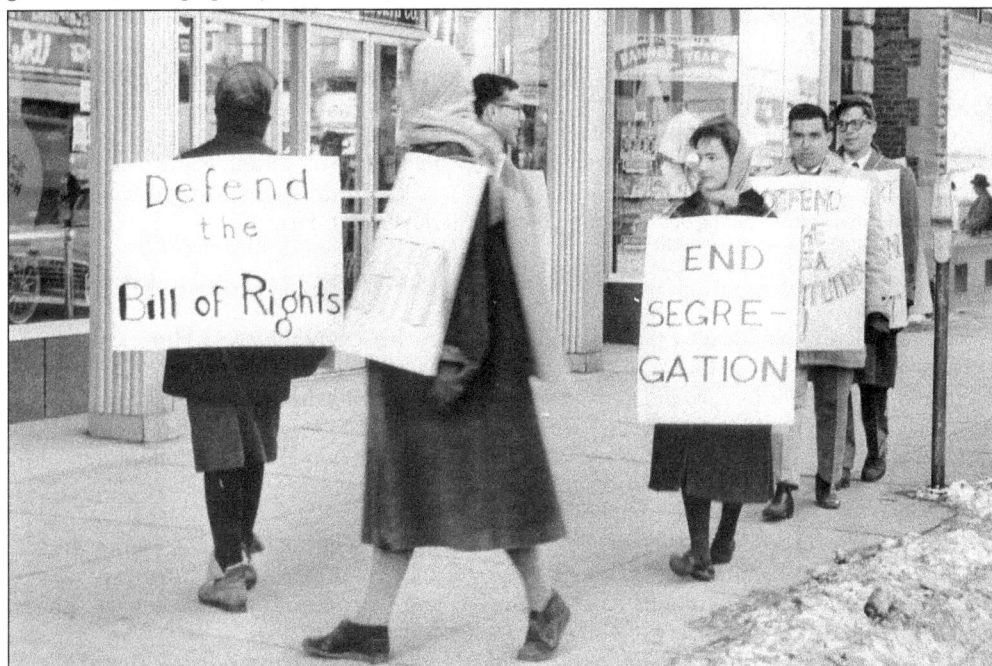

Picketers outside Woolworth's department store on East State Street wear signs supporting sit-ins at Woolworth stores taking place in the South. The sit-ins were in protest of segregation at Woolworth lunch counters. The Cornell University students picketing here in 1960 were members of the Cornell Committee Against Segregation.

BIBLIOGRAPHY

Abt, Henry E. *Ithaca*. Ithaca, NY: Ross W. Kellogg, 1926.

Allmon, Warren D., and Robert M. Ross. *Ithaca is Gorges: A Guide to the Geology of the Ithaca Area*. Ithaca, NY: The Paleontological Research Institution, 1998.

Armstead, Myra B. Young, et al. *A Heritage Uncovered: The Black Experience in Upstate New York 1800–1925*. Elmira, NY: Chemung County Historical Society, 1988.

Bishop, Morris. *A History of Cornell*. Ithaca, NY: Cornell University Press, 1962.

Burns, Thomas W. *Initial Ithacans*. Ithaca, NY: Press of the Ithaca Journal, 1904.

Burritt, Joseph C. *With a Jeweler's Eye: The Photographs of Joseph C. Burritt*. Ithaca, NY: DeWitt Historical Society of Tompkins County, 1988.

Clarke, Frank W. *Views Around Ithaca*. Ithaca, NY: Andrus, McChain & Co., 1869.

Dieckmann, Jane M. *A Short History of Tompkins County*. Ithaca, NY: DeWitt Historical Society of Tompkins County, 1986.

Dieckmann, Jane M., ed. *The Towns of Tompkins County: From Podunk to the Magnetic Springs*. Ithaca, NY: DeWitt Historical Society of Tompkins County, 1998.

Harcourt, John B. *The Ithaca College Story*. Ithaca, NY: Ithaca College, 1983.

Hesch, Merrill, and Richard Pieper. Revised and updated by Harry Littell. *Ithaca Then & Now*. Ithaca, NY: McBooks Press, 2000.

Kammen, Carol. *The Peopling of Tompkins County*. Interlaken, NY: Heart of the Lakes Publishing, 1985.

Kaplin, Colleen M. *Take Two: A Guide to Ithaca's Movie Making Past*. Ithaca, NY: Isidore Stephanus Sons, 1989.

Norris, W. Glenn. *Old Indian Trails in Tompkins County*. Ithaca, NY: DeWitt Historical Society of Tompkins County, 1944.

Norris, W. Glenn. *The Origin of Place Names in Tompkins County*. Ithaca, NY: DeWitt Historical Society of Tompkins County, 1951.

Sisler, Carol U. *Cayuga Lake: Past, Present, and Future*. Ithaca, NY: Enterprise Publishing, 1989.

Sisler, Carol U. *Enterprising Families, Ithaca, New York: Their Houses and Businesses*. Ithaca, NY: DeWitt Historical Society of Tompkins County, 2002.

Sisler, Carol U. et al., ed. *Ithaca's Neighborhoods: The Rhine, the Hill, and the Goose Pasture*. Ithaca, NY: DeWitt Historical Society of Tompkins County, 1988.

Snodderly, Daniel R. *Ithaca and Its Past: The History and Architecture of the Downtown*. Ithaca, NY: DeWitt Historical Society of Tompkins County, 1982.

Spencer, Spence, ed. *The Scenery of Ithaca and the Head Waters of Cayuga Lake*. Ithaca, NY: S. Spencer, 1866.

INDEX

Visit us at
arcadiapublishing.com
···

www.ingramcontent.com/pod-product-compliance
Lightning Source LLC
Chambersburg PA
CBHW050638110426
42813CB00007B/1853